THE GIRL WITHOUT A NAME

OTHER NOVELS WRITTEN BY STUART P. COATES

Norma Jeane's Wishes in Time	(2008) iUniverse
Marilyn's Mindset	(2010) iUniverse
Whispers across Time	(2012) iUniverse
Earth Grid Down	(2017) iUniverse

THE GIRL WITHOUT A NAME

The MUSE *of* MONTAGUA

STUART P. COATES

iUniverse®

THE GIRL WITHOUT A NAME
THE MUSE OF MONTAGUA

iUniverse books may be ordered through booksellers or by contacting:

iUniverse
1663 Liberty Drive
Bloomington, IN 47403
www.iuniverse.com
1-800-Authors (1-800-288-4677)

ISBN: 978-1-5320-9139-1 (sc)
ISBN: 978-1-5320-9138-4 (hc)
ISBN: 978-1-5320-9137-7 (e)

Print information available on the last page.

iUniverse rev. date: 01/14/2020

A VERY SPECIAL NOTE OF ACKNOWLEDGMENT AND THANK YOU

This story was inspired by the artwork imagery of a very talented artist and very dear friend.

Dear Barbarann,

This book will be coming out in publication somewhere around a very special day. Here is your birthday present. Happy Birthday!

It is slightly longer than a card. Have fun reading a story based on a character you drew up!

The character that you created with butterfly wings gets her own story and finally gets the chance to fly.

"Buckle up! It's going to be a bumpy ride!"

With all my best wishes and love, your friend,

Stuart

THE CAST OF CHARACTERS

Captain Archibald Crane ... Captain of the *HMS Venture,* who discovers an unknown land deep within the earth in the year 1875 after his ship has been commissioned for polar exploration by Queen Victoria.

Ageyutsa ... The main character in the story, a girl who has lost her memory, she falls down a deep, dark entrance into an unknown land where all animals and insects live forever and can speak.

Hootie ... The talking owl, and faithful companion, who finds Ageyutsa on the surface world and leads her on the greatest adventure of her lifetime.

General Cornelius ... The head of the owls (who are the military guards) and decides to name this foreigner from the surface world Ageyutsa.

The Hermit on Eternity Mountain ... The Great Spirit who is rumored to be the creator of all.

Charlie the disgruntled cherub, trains Ageyutsa in using her new abilities as the first female archangel.

Mordock ... A sorcerer and an expert with the bow, he is a fallen archangel, and the son of Lucifer.

Enchantra ... A sorceress, she is the wife of Mordock.

INTRODUCTION

Let us step into the mind of God, the Almighty Creator of the entire universe. How and where, exactly, if you were God, the Almighty creator of everything, could and would He hide the Garden of Eden from the human race? He did not destroy it, he hid it. The Garden of Eden was forever self renewing. It was immune to the ravages of time. God could not destroy the Garden of Eden any more than he could destroy Himself. There was too much of God already in it. The only way God could destroy the Garden of Eden would be to destroy the earth itself.

God has not destroyed the earth, and since the Garden of Eden was forever renewing itself, He has not destroyed the Garden of Eden.

But, He has hidden it from all of mankind. That much is certain because of the fact that even with all of our satellite technology and scientific advancements, with every inch of the surface of the globe having been surveyed through exploration or technology, we have not discovered it.

So, where is it? It must exist upon the earth because of the Garden of Eden's very God-given, ever-renewing nature. It was eternal.

We have half of the story — the creation of the Garden of Eden. We know that the first man and first woman, Adam and Eve, were cast out of the Garden of Eden upon eating the fruit of the Tree of Knowledge, which was forbidden to do by God.

We also know that once Adam and Eve were cast out of the Garden of Eden, God concealed the Garden from Mankind.

But, we are still lacking enough information to locate its whereabouts.

Perhaps more clues are available in the Holy Bible. According to the Book of Matthew, there are 14 generations between the time of Adam and the time of Noah. We also know of The Great Flood during the time of Noah. Noah, of course, was the one who built the ark just before the Great Flood.

About the Great Flood, one question has been rarely asked — when the flooding of the earth ceased, where did the water go?

The water that had flooded the earth towered above every mountain on the planet's surface, according to the Scriptures.

Evaporation of all that seawater would have taken centuries, if not millennia. So it didn't happen that way. So, this one question still remains — where did the water go?

The science of archaeology may help answer this question. According to much archaeological evidence, we also know that the earth was once much smaller in its volume than it is in present day.

There was once a singular landmass called Pangaea. It split apart, many millennia ago, and these fragments from the singular landmass formed the seven known continents of today's world. The earth effectively expanded.

Hypothesis: Perhaps the expansion of our old world took place soon after the flood?

It is an interesting hypothesis because this would certainly explain where the water went. It would have been redistributed over the planet's surface as the original continent of Pangaea broke up into its seven smaller fragments, allowing the waters to be drained down these newly formed cavities, forming the seas and oceans; with the smaller land fragments later becoming the seven known continents of today's expanded, much larger Earth.

This concept would also conform to the ancient histories and old Indian legends of how the original Native Peoples of North America and South America were settled in this part of the world over land bridges.

Pangaea was a single continent. Everything was joined together at one time.

As Pangaea broke up, there were land bridges that existed between what was then the European continent and what is now North America.

Also, there was a similar land bridge between South America and North America. It still exists today. It is called Mexico.

However, the original land bridge between the European continent and the North American continent broke apart as the world expanded during the last ice age, 18,900 years ago.

The original Indian tribes had established themselves on North America through what is now known as Canada, and they then migrated south; while other Indian tribes migrated north from South America, through the land bridge that is now Mexico and into what is now known as the southern United States.

Now, just for the sake of argument, many, many millennia ago, say the Garden of Eden lay buried by the Great Flood of Noah's time, buried by God, on the western shores of Pangaea, before it broke up.

We know that the Garden of Eden would have been on the western shore due to The Genesis referencing the location of where Cain and Abel established themselves East of Eden.

This would place the Garden of Eden, buried deep within the central North Western portion of Pangaea, or what is now known as the continent of North America.

Nothing ever died in the Garden of Eden. Plants, insects and animals, Man and Woman in their earliest forms, lived forever, as long as they remained in the Garden.

There was no concept of time in the Garden of Eden. What of the animals? What of the insects? What of the plants?

What if the Garden of Eden had become a once-hidden-by-God, subterranean-world-onto-its-own, and God placed it deep within the earth by the sheer weight of the waters of the Great Flood itself to hide it from all of mankind?

What if the Garden of Eden was uncovered in today's world? Purely by accident, of course; but, just for the sake of argument, what if the Garden of Eden really did exist and it was rediscovered?

What if that hidden, subterranean world, a world where time had no meaning, where there was no death, where one would not age, was rediscovered in our own modern times?

PROLOGUE

After all of this discussion of God and Creation, we, being only human, naturally, by our very human natures, begin this story by telling a lie; or rather, a concealment of the truth... a hidden message within a message, a message containing a secret code.

Recall the secret, coded messages from World War II. A message would be written about a certain subject, but the contents of the message would have held some sort of secret meaning, and upon its reception, to be decoded and its actual meaning later derived.

It was a practice in operation long before World War II — and such was the case with the following message from a certain Archibald Crane, a highly experienced Captain aboard her Majesty Queen Victoria's, *The Venture* an exploratory, seagoing vessel in the latter half of the 19th century.

The message below was conveyed to the Admiralty. On the surface, the message was written during circumnavigation of the world by ship and was with regard to the actual circumference of the globe, but its true meaning lay hidden, later to be decoded. The ship's log was sent to the Admiralty and from there, they would decode Crane's hidden message.

July 7, 1875

On behalf of her Majesty Queen Victoria, I write the following to preserve our rather lengthy voyage for posterity...

The True Form and Magnitude of the Earth

The Facts and experiments already advanced render undeniable that the surface of all the waters of the earth is horizontal that however irregular the upper outline of the land itself maybe the whole mass of land and water together constitutes an immense, non-moving, circular plane.

If we travel by land or sea from any part of the earth in the direction of any Meridian line and towards the northern central star called Polaris, we come to one in the same place a region of ice, where the star which has been our guide is directly above us or vertical to our position. This region is really the center of the earth and recent observations seem to prove that it is a vast central tidal sea nearly a thousand miles in diameter and surrounded by a great wall or barrier of ice eighty to a hundred miles in breadth if from the central region we trace the outline of down to the lands which projector radiates from it and the surface of which is above the water, we find that the present form of the earth or dry land as distinguished from the waters of the great deep is in a regular mass of capes, bays and islands terminating in great Bluffs or headlands projecting principally towards the south or at least in a direction away from the great northern center.

If we now sail with our backs continually to the central star Polaris nearly the center of the Earth's surface we shall arrive at another region of ice upon whatever Meridian we sail keeping the northern center behind us we are checked in our progress by vast and lofty cliffs of ice.

If we turn to the right or to the left of our meridian, I see barriers beset us during the whole of our passage hence we have found that there is a great ebbing and flowing sea at the Earth's center with a boundary wall of ice nearly a hundred miles in thickness and three thousand miles in circumference that springing or projecting from this icy wall irregular masses of land stretch out towards the south where a desolate waste of turbulent waters surrounds the continents and is itself in girdled by vast belts and packs of ice bounded by immense frozen barriers the lateral depth and extent of which are utterly unknown.

Sincerely, Archibald Crane, Captain of The Venture, this July 7, 1875.

It was a message that, on the surface, regarding the overall size of the globe as our planet Earth, seemed rather boring and mundane in its contents. It read as though it was a message about circumnavigation, on the surface, but in truth, upon decoding, the good Captain Crane was seeking an entry way into a subterranean world within our own world.

There was this 19th century theory that the earth was hollow and Captain Crane, his ship and his crew, along with the

Admiralty were trekking to Antarctica, seeking a passageway by sea into that hidden, subterranean world that lay beneath our own.

Captain Crane, along with his ship and crew, went missing on this last known voyage.

His real mission was to seek out and rediscover a place once known as Eden. *The Venture* sailed as far south is Antarctica, past the last known barrier reef of ice and snow, the temperature began to warm, quite considerably, and a massive fog was seen on the horizon, which had kept obscured a massive opening into the very earth's crust and which led downward, ever downward, o'er thousands upon thousands of miles, not quite at the vertical, but nevertheless, in such a steep descent, the ship was never able to turn hard about to reverse its course from said descent in which the ship and crew and its Captain were now trapped in, and in which they sailed into, each of the crew of *The Venture* was forever consumed by the fog, and they were never heard from by the entire human race ever again.

Almost 150 years have passed since Captain Crane was commissioned by Queen Victoria to seek out this hidden land of the Antarctic also known as the Eden of which the Holy Bible speaks. In all that time, the secret entranceway discovered by Captain Crane has remained hidden, and although there have been some outlandish theories being raised about the earth being hollow over many centuries, clear, absolute proof has never been confirmed, nor truly established – yet.

The Land of Eden was massive. Could there possibly be more than one entrance? There was a route entrance at the

South Pole, according to Crane's Ship's Log. Perhaps, there is an identical entrance at the North Pole?

Another entrance to Earth's core would soon be discovered, not in the year 1875, but on the other side of the globe, and in our modern times, in our present day – by a young female mountaineer, whose sense of adventure would bring her to the very center of the earth itself.

She would undergo the strangest of transformations by merely coming into physical contact with certain insects, the fallows in the air, and even become a new species, never before seen on the earth below nor in the heavens above, for she would be one of only very few human beings to ever come into physical contact and touch the robe of the Great Spirit, also known as God.

CHAPTER 1
ASCENT

Mt. Denali, Denali National Park and Preserve, Alaska, USA, current ascent altitude: 15,263 feet and climbing.

Oxygen deprivation — it can do strange things to people. She could not remember her name, not even her own name. Extreme altitudes produce such an effect on the mind. The air was so thin at this altitude; it felt like she was on another planet.

All she was seeing was white — snow white — the kind of white found on mountain peaks, especially on this one, one of the largest mountains in the world. It felt like another world had appeared at this altitude.

It truly felt like Mars.

She always liked shiny things — sunrises over high mountaintops, sparkling jewelry, diamonds, and glittering clothing, gadgets, especially of the high-tech variety.

She was also a bit of a kleptomaniac.

In simpler language, she was a thief. But this was not exactly how she thought of herself.

She just took shiny things, without asking permission – anyone's permission, whether it was from an individual, or from a high-profile corporation like NASA.

She liked the suit. It was shiny and she took it without asking. That didn't really make her a thief, just someone that omitted to ask permission. In her eyes, it was just an oversight. She needed it. The suit served a purpose.

She was making her attempted ascent in a stolen NASA spacesuit, design for the Martian environment. The suit would inflate itself if she were in a freefall the suit's motion sensors would detect.

She had stolen the suit from the Kennedy Space Center in Florida, eluded detection of the motion sensors and security guards, and had snuck into the main laboratory.

The Mars landing mission had proven, conclusively, and once and for all, that the earth was round. All of those images from outer space transmitted by the early Martian probes — Earth was definitely not flat, earth was a globe.

And, of course, there were the moon missions in the 1960s and 1970s. Mankind had gone to the moon in 1969, but then, there was still so much to be explored on our own planet, so much was still unknown, lying hidden from sight, or perhaps just beyond our reach, perhaps under the earth.

Admiral Byrd had been wrong in the 1950s. Over a half-century earlier, he declared that the earth was flat and hollow.

The earth was not flat, that half he had gotten incorrect, but what about the other half of his conjecture, was he only half wrong?

Was the earth hollow and that one could enter the interior of the planet at either of its poles?

She was getting close, very close, to the North Pole at this point.

She was also putting her life in extreme danger - solo climbing the third largest mountain in the world, or rather on the surface of the world, Mt. Denali, in the harsh climate of Alaska.

If she could only reach the summit — she was only a little over 9000 feet away from it, as one would measure by altitude — and she had acclimated herself, as best as she could, against the thinning atmosphere, against the cold.

About the cold — it was not her concern, not in this suit that she was wearing. It was a spacesuit from NASA — its assumed design was for the conditions of the planet Mars, with a special safety feature.

If she were to slip, lose her footing and begin tumbling down the mountainside, the safety features of this outfit would protect her by inflating the entire suit, much like the Mars Land Rover. It was housed in a protective, inflatable outer shell, designed to soft-land from a Martian orbit.

Her suit would inflate to over 15 times its present volume and she would roll down the mountainside as if contained inside a beach ball. Rolling down the third largest mountain in the world — or on the world, if Byrd's theory would turn out to be correct — would be the wildest ride even beyond that of the largest roller coaster, but she would remain unharmed to the fall.

She clicked on the air supply hoses. She had almost forgotten that the suit contained an internal emergency tank of oxygen and her head began to clear.

She could now make it to the summit. All she had to do was climb at a reasonable, steady pace.

The suit was most assuredly protecting her from the cold. It was conditioned for over 100 below Fahrenheit and an extremely thin atmosphere, as was found on Mars. The suit was ideal for her current surroundings, if she didn't get 20 years in San Quentin by getting caught on orbital satellite camera wearing it.

She was now nearing the summit and far below her she could see a massive depression going down into the earth itself, from this vantage point, now that she was literally almost on top of the world.

It was several miles away from her current location, but it was there.

The Admiral had been correct many decades ago — it was possible to enter into the planet Earth from either of its poles.

The entrance ways were hidden by dense fogs, but she had found one of them, miles away from her, but it was there. It was there! It was no illusion. It was no hallucination.

She stood there, on the summit of the mountain, bending at the waist and falling to her hands and knees, trying to regroup, trying to catch her breath. The climb had been worth it. She had discovered a part of the world no other human being had ever seen. The earth was not flat, but it was hollow. By God, it was hollow!

She took out her cell phone and began photographing the expanse before her and the huge depression, as photographic proof of her find.

Suddenly, as if shaken by the hand of God itself, the entire mountain began to tremble.

Earthquake!

Alaska was renowned for having them — and here she was on the peak of the largest mountain in the state.

The surface she was standing upon began to give way. She was losing control of her footing! She had mere seconds to put away her cell phone.

To perform a descent of the mountain was now completely out of the question, but she had a really crazy idea. An almost-insane one!

She inflated the suit by activating its emergency Mars landing safety features.

She would now have to test the suit to its absolute limit. An escape was necessary. She would deliberately attempt to roll down the mountain from its summit sliding on the snow in the training suit like a toboggan.

CHAPTER 2
OLD BACK ROADS

All owls speak. It is a well-known fact that owls will speak. They speak to all upon or *within* the earth.

Butterflies, of course, cannot speak; and this is also a well-known fact. Butterflies communicate in another way. They speak to us with the flutter of their wings.

It is all a matter of perception. Perception is the key to all understanding, to all creatures that inhabit this world.

Owls and butterflies can speak, just as well as humans do, in their own unique, most perceptible way, if someone takes the time to listen.

Owls are wise creatures of the night and Butterflies are wise creatures of the day. The Owls and the Butterflies — all creatures of the world — are equally important on the face of the earth, or *under* it, to the Great Spirit, the Creator of all living things.

Perhaps it is already known that the Eagles can also speak, just as well as the Owls do, in plain, ordinary North American English.

About the Eagles, I should not have mentioned them yet. I'm getting ahead of myself.

You see, there was this young woman, a most beautiful, young woman, with the longest, prettiest braids of blonde hair, with the most majestic of green eyes ... and she was falling down this deep, mile-after-mile, dark, rocky entranceway on a hillside, here in the green, dense, lush forest, a secretive, hidden region of the woods that was guarded by swarms of enormous butterflies for thousands upon thousands of our years.

To properly perceive the entranceway, close your eyes. Seek. Search through the blackness, down, deep down, through the darkened, half hidden by green foliage passageway that you will see forming before you.

Allow a moment for your eyes to begin to adjust to the darkness, let your mind's imagination begin to expand, allow your mind to widen its perception.

Permit your mind to fly on wings, as does the butterfly, as does the owl, as does the eagle. Pierce through the darkness.

Now… open your eyes once more.

There it is, down, down, far down, at the end of the long passageway.

See it through the darkness? It is in an unknown forest, a forest you have never before explored, in a forgotten corridor of the mind.

It is a doorway, a passageway, a gateway, if you will, from one world into another — from this world's outer surface, through this very long connecting tunnel, into a hidden world, a world from long ago, an underworld once described to her as a child, a young child — the old, very old, the ancient Indian legends — the inner, subterranean world of Montagua.

She became conscious once more, awakening, as if from a dream. Tumbling head over heels, for thousands of times, staying just ahead of the miniature avalanche that was forming behind her, she felt no pain being fully protected in the inflated Martian spacesuit.

But it was the helmet. She hadn't planned on the consequences of wearing the helmet. Her head was being rattled around inside as if it was a peanut in its shell. She was lapsing in and out of consciousness, punch-drunk, much like a boxer; she was numb from the blows to her head.

She didn't feel any pain and that strange tale of Montagua, the ancient Indian story of the world being hollow, as told through her family, through the generations and generations.

She was part Cherokee. The Cherokee legend of Montagua — the story told to her as a child by her mother so many years earlier.

These were the thoughts that were going through her mind as she tumbled down the mountain rolling to a stop at its base.

She had fallen over 17,000 feet in altitude, nearly 4 miles of descent; tumbling, ever tumbling, rolling head over heels without end in that inflated circular Martian spacesuit.

It had mimicked exactly the same sort of bouncing affect of how the early space probes had descended through the Martian atmosphere on the planet 30 years earlier.

Instead of a probe's vital equipment being protected by the outer rubbery layers she was the cargo. Her body was what was being protected, but she hadn't counted on the effects of the helmet. Its layers of protection were sadly inadequate, that much was certain.

It wasn't oxygen deprivation this time — she couldn't remember her name. There were only fragments of memories.

She was experiencing amnesia.

She couldn't remember anything about her life, not in the present, only in the past.

All that was going through her mind was the ancient story of Montagua that her mother had once described to her when she was a young child. She had remembered those old bedtime stories that her mother used to tell her for years. Now, these stories were the only things present in her mind.

They were the only memories she could remember about her life — those early childhood Indian legend stories; and this unknown voice, a voice calling to her from what seemed to be the mountain.

"Ageyutsa. Ageyutsa. Ageyutsa, come to me."

Ageyutsa — it was the Cherokee word for girl — and it kept repeating that old Cherokee word. Ageyutsa, Ageyutsa, Ageyutsa, active and calling to her as if it were her name.

"Ageyutsa. Ageyutsa. Ageyutsa, come forth. Come to me."

She saw a vehicle ahead, parked on the side of the road, just off the gravel, and she remembered that it was her red Mustang. But she could not remember her name. She remembered it was her car, but she couldn't remember her name.

She slowly staggered to her feet. She was covered half in snow, half in dirt from the mile after mile tumble. She had rolled all the way down the mountain, but the suit had saved her life — for what little, few fragments of her life she could now remember.

The area seemed familiar. Alaska. She knew she was in Alaska and she knew she had been here before, many times.

This was familiar territory to her, but she couldn't remember her name. She removed the helmet from her and threw it on the ground, still quite disoriented and dizzy.

"Ageyutsa. Ageyutsa. Ageyutsa, come to me."

She turned back to face the mountain, and yelled at it, "Shut up, you old ghost. You're not real. You're not here."

She was steadying herself on her feet now. She was regaining her composure.

She staggered to the car and steadied herself upon it, pulling herself around to the driver's side, she opened the door and collapsed into the front seat, pulling her legs in behind her and shutting the door.

"I've got to get away! I've got to get away from here! I'll go to a place you will never find me, you old ghost!"

She fiddled with the ignition. She looked at the manual stick shift beside her and put it in neutral and turned the ignition key once more.

The Mustang's engine fired to life. She put the car in its lowest gear and gradually began to pull away from where she had parked, through the lightly grassed field, and back onto the road. She stepped on the gas pedal.

The car began to accelerate and she shifted into its second gear, leaving the backdrop of the mountain behind her in her rear-view mirror.

Third gear. Another shift. Fourth gear.

She shifted into overdrive at over 70 miles an hour. The rpm's and initial roar of the engine were subsiding and she was pulling away from the mountain, but the voice kept following her in her head.

"Ageyutsa, Ageyutsa, Ageyutsa!"

CHAPTER 3

THE OWL WHO SPOKE

Her Mustang convertible came to a screeching halt. There was a loud POP, followed by the most distinctive hissing sound. That darned owl had just punctured her car's front right tire. Using what appeared to be a menacing weapon of some sort, sporting a sharp metal tip at one end of it. He had punctured the tire, tearing a large, open gash through it.

He was the largest of owls she had ever seen. He stood nearly 3 feet tall, measuring almost up to her waist, marching up and down in front of her automobile; holding what looked like a weapon tucked under one wing.

He had been strutting, with a most direct and intentional purpose, like a soldier, up and down the road, deliberately blocking her way.

He was attempting to mimic the sound of a snare drum as he marched, left-to-right, turning in the opposite direction and resuming his marching, directly in her path.

He loudly voiced, in tandem with each step he took, pausing briefly at the end of each marching line, rotating and then resuming his rhythmic step.

"Par ... Rahm – Pahm – Pahm– Pahm...

"Par ... Rahm –Pahm – Pahm– Pahm...

"Par ... Rahm –Pahm."

He stopped motionless in his tracks, bringing himself to attention and loudly shouting into the air, "AABOUUUUT FACE!"

The huge owl had rotated himself at a right angle to the automobile and pointed what appeared to be his weapon which he had used to impale the car's tire directly at her, giving a stern stare.

"HALT! You are trespassing on private territory! Speak your purpose, human."

He briefly looked upward, over the hood of the automobile, directly looking at her still sitting half shocked at his size and at the weapon he was carrying, which, now that she was closer to him, she perceived it to be an old-fashioned rifle, fashioned in the late 18th century, made at around the time of the Revolutionary War era, complete with a very sharp bayonet secured on its end.

He threw his head back momentarily gazing at the sky above as he asked in a loud voice, "Whoooo in heaven…."

He brought is head back to his straight stare at her, finishing his question, "…are you?"

His voice startled her. This huge owl, this creature of the woods, actually spoke. He spoke in her language. He was speaking English!

She had been driving down an old back road, taking a well-known shortcut, one of many that she knew. She would have gone through anything to beat the traffic, anything but him!

She sat in her car in complete bewilderment, shutting off the engine, opening the door and slowly moving toward him to get a closer look.

"An owl? You're a huge owl?"

"Correct!"

She stammered as she replied under her breath, "I'm sure he —" as she began thinking to herself aloud, but then she realized, to be more polite, she should try to speak to him, directly ask of him the most obvious question.

"You can talk? I mean — you — you — can speak?"

"All owls speak, if you ever bothered to listen," he replied.

"No, they don't."

"That's because you never listen!" he replied to her, his owl equivalent of eyebrows pushing downward on his head. The expressions upon his face were almost human.

"Never listen?"

How did he possibly know that she rarely would listen to anyone?

She tried again to open a dialogue with him by asking another question.

"What are you?"

"Isn't that obvious? I am an owl."

"I can *see* that you are!" she said to him, still in amazement. "But, you are the largest I have ever seen! Never have I heard one speak. Who are you?"

"*That was* going to be my question to you. Whoooo are you?"

She replied in a defiant tone, "I'm not telling you. My name is not important, but what you did to my car is! Look at this tire. You sliced right through it! You slashed it! How dare you. Why?"

"I had to stop you. The Great Spirit told me that you could be a problem. Even so, we need your hands."

"My hands?"

"Yes, those outer limbs of yours — you have four fingers and a thumb on each of the two uppermost, for grasping things. You call them — hands. They will be most useful. We have not had one such as you with hands, in my country, for the longest of times."

He smiled, as he thought back, placing his left wing under his beak while thinking back, as a human being might do in a gesture of rubbing his chin while recalling a memory of some sort. This owl was smiling, just like a human being.

"We have had one such as you in my home, a long time ago. You are the female of your species. You are what are known as a woman."

The owl cleared his throat, "The — a-hem — man was similar, but different to you. It has been a very long time, practically, since the Beginning, since a woman has been in Montagua. Montagua was known by another name back at the Beginning. It could prove to be..."

The owl paused in thought for a moment.

"Different. Perhaps even ... interesting. Perhaps ... exciting.

The owl spoke up, "Yes, Montagua could use some excitement."

The owl went silent and thought to himself, "She would become an excellent Muse. Yes, a Muse of Montagua. Montagua could use a Muse. This one would be an excellent choice."

He once again smiled at her as he again spoke.

"There once was the other of your species, what you call a man. He visited Montagua, a long time ago. He gave me this," he said to her, presenting his weapon to her for her to inspect as he continued to explain, "to defend this perimeter."

The owl could see that she held a great interest in his weapon. As a gesture of good faith, he tried to gain her trust.

"I see you are interested in this. I will allow you to examine it, but please be careful with what you say while holding it. All is not what it appears to be."

The woman responded, "What do you mean? I know how to handle a rifle. Is it loaded?"

"Not with powder or projectiles. It contains something else, something far more powerful. I'd better not tell you.

"All I ask is that you handle it delicately, with extreme care. Be careful what you say while holding it."

The owl lifted what appeared to be the rifle with both wings and held the weapon horizontally in front of her for her to more closely inspect.

He then went on to further explain, "The Woods holds many wonders within it. I am to guard it. I was ordered by the man. He was a Captain of a ship. It is my duty. A long time ago, the man, he taught me how to march, and how to hold this as I do. He gave me this — this thing."

He presented the weapon he was carrying to her. It appeared to be an old-fashioned, a very old-fashioned rifle. It indeed had a bayonet attached to the end of the barrel. It was the sort of rifle that had not been used in over two centuries.

Even though the rifle was very old, it obviously had been kept in pristine condition. She briefly opened the firing chamber. The owl had been telling the truth. The chamber on the rifle was empty. It held no projectiles to fire from it, but there was this sweet odor that she was now detecting that had escaped from the rifle. She involuntarily inhaled the sweetest of fragrances.

She began feeling slightly dizzy, disoriented. She briefly shook her head and began to regain her composure. The dizziness was only there for a moment, only temporary, but she was feeling very different, it was almost like a hunger or perhaps a thirst. She wasn't sure, perhaps both a hunger and a thirst combined; and she was beginning to feel this annoying, uncontrollable itch developing just below both shoulder blades on her back.

Her examination of the rifle was distracted when she heard…

"Par ... Rahm – Pahm – Pahm– Pahm.

"Par ... Rahm – Pahm – Pahm– Pahm."

The owl had resumed his marching up and down in front of her. Realizing the rifle was empty, incapable of firing any bullets, she smirked, giving the rifle one more look-over, now realizing that it was relatively harmless, she decided to hand him back his weapon. He looked rather lost without it. He seemed to be off in his rhythm, out of sync.

She placed the rifle on her shoulder with the barrel pointing behind her at her car.

She whispered to herself, "Back in the day they made this rifle, it was probably meant to stop a carriage, not a car.

"But that bayonet sure did its job on my tire!"

She thought to herself and then more softly but more audibly spoke under her breath while still holding the rifle with its barrel pointing backward at her automobile, "Many years ago, they called a car a horseless carriage."

Unknown to her, starlets of sparkling energy began shooting out of the barrel just as she mentioned the word carriage. Her vehicle began to transform in its appearance.

The itch on her back was becoming more intense and most annoying. Little did she realize that two large black patches were forming parallel to each other along her back. What appeared to be wings were slowly sprouting. She, of course, could not see this. The appendages were also too small for even the owl to perceive all in these early stages of what was really happening to her.

She smiled at the way he was trying to compensate for his inability to establish himself.

"Here," she said smiling, "you might as well have your rifle back. You look rather — let's just say, out of place without it."

She then said to the owl, "Did you know your rifle was giving off a very peculiar odor?"

The owl made a military maneuver in the middle of his march.

"ABOOOUT FACE!"

They briefly looked at each other and both smiled. The owl had suddenly realized what she had said.

"Did you just say my rifle gave off an odor?"

She replied, "Un-huh. I have never smelled something so sweet. And now I seem to have the strangest feeling — an itch on two places on my back, just below the shoulder blades. It is the funniest feeling."

She was starting to look younger in appearance.

The owl immediately thought to himself, "Oh-oh!", as he was now looking behind her at what had been her automobile and now her very noticeable youthful appearance. She looked as young as perhaps someone in her early 20s.

She brought the rifle to a vertical position and presented to the owl his rifle. The owl courteously responded by accepting it and seemed to breathe a sigh of relief. With the rifle returned to him he once again seemed whole, completed.

The woman hesitated and then said, "You are much larger than any owl I have ever seen in my entire life."

The owl replied, "Most creatures on the surface of this world do seem smaller. I have noted that as well. Many on this surface world are not at all like they are in Montagua."

"You keep mentioning Montagua. What is a Montagua?" questioned the woman.

He had to get her away from here. She had been infected. Knowing the sweet odor that she had just mentioned, the owl knew that she would soon become contagious.

He would have to use his trickery to have her follow him. And he also knew that she shouldn't touch him in any way while in her present state.

She now unknowingly possessed an uncontrollable, chameleon-like ability. Touching him would mean that she could easily acquire his abilities and attributes as an owl.

She could most likely transform into part owl, part human, even larger in size, strength, faster and more manoeuvrable in flight than he was.

In truth, in her present condition, after having smelled the spores hidden inside of the rifle, it was not just the owl who is in danger of her obtaining his abilities, it was *any living creature* with which she would have physical contact, she would acquire their abilities, partially their appearance, and their attributes.

The side effects were becoming more noticeable. She appeared to be 10 years younger than she had been moments earlier and growing younger with each passing second. She was becoming practically eternal, filled with youth and ever-renewing vitality.

She would remain in this contagious state and un-aging for at least the next several millennia. There was no known cure, only time, and a great deal of it was needed.

The fragrance had come from spores which had fallen into the rifle through its barrel which had been leaning up against what was once recorded in the Bible, in The First Book of Moses: The Genesis, as the "Tree of Life".

He would have to reveal just enough information to lure her away, before she realized what was happening to her now regenerating, now perfecting, youthful body now directly tapping into the limitless energy of her eternal soul.

She would soon discover the changes that were occurring to her outward appearance and they could not be explained on this surface world.

He would have to get her to follow him.

"Montagua is my home... I guess you would now call it a country up on here, the surface."

"I have never heard of a country called Montagua."

"Montagua is larger than this country — much larger. It is the largest country under the world."

"Did you just say — *under*? What did you mean by on the surface of *this* world?"

"Montagua is far below this outer shell's forest surface. It is very old, not that *old* has much meaning, for time does not pass here as it does in Montagua. Montagua's time moves much slower. It is a much easier, more forgiving time.

"You have occurrences which are very strange here on this surface world.

"They are known as deaths. There never has been anything such as a death in Montagua, only here. Only on this surface world does one experience such a thing. But not in Montagua."

"Everything must die — eventually."

"Not in Montagua. Would you like to see it? It is approximately 1 mile in that direction.

"Of course, if you are scared of the woods...? But if you want to live the adventure of a lifetime, restore your youth to its prime, see a place where time has very little meaning, all you have to do is follow me.

"Would you like to be young again and live ... forever?"

"Forever? Don't be ridiculous! Nothing can live forever."

"Not up here, not in this world, but in Montagua, it is possible. There are wonders beyond your imagination — far beyond your human existence, far below what is here. Or, are you afraid?"

Without warning, the owl, flung the rifle over his back and went aloft and across the skies, circling her, taunting her. The young woman, startled by his sudden departure, gazed upward into the sky, slightly covering her eyes from the sun.

Her eyes returned to the ground once more and then she realized what had happened during the conversation she'd had with the owl, her automobile it been changed into a carriage, an old fashion 17th century carriage. Just the carriage, a carriage without horses, literally, a horseless carriage.

She had said the words "horseless carriage" while pointing the barrel of the rifle in the direction of her automobile and this had been the result. A carriage, but without horses! The rifle had the properties of a magical wand. She was going nowhere!

She screamed, "My car! What happened to my car?!? My Mustang convertible!"

She opened the carriage door on the left-hand side of the vehicle, still in shock, looking at its interior in total disbelief, and growing all the more annoyed at the constant, persistent itching on her back that she could not reach to scratch.

She whispered under her breath, "What has that owl done to my car? I'm sure he's responsible! Somehow, I just know he's responsible for this! We'll just see who's afraid!"

She began pursuing the owl overhead on foot, leaping off the narrow, gravel roadway and into the woods she went.

The owl looked down at the tiny dot-like figure of the woman far below him almost with a pleasing smile that he had persuaded her to follow him as he flew off in the direction that he needed to go to travel further into the woods and to return to his home.

She was fleet of foot, but she could barely keep pace with the owl who continued his flight overhead.

The incessant itching on her back was driving her almost insane. She reached for a tree branch, broke it off and every 20 to 30 yards, she would cease running, bring herself to a full stop, contort and twist herself by reaching over and behind her head and neck with the branch and desperately start scratching the middle of her back with the branch in order to bring some form of relief. However, doing so caused her to begin to lose her pace with keeping up with the owl.

The owl thought to himself, "This will never do," and he shouted down to her from above, "You must learn to fly like I do, if you are to escape the dense woods! Prepare yourself! You must join me in the air!"

She yelled back at him, "You rodent-eating, feathered little freak! Get back down here and bring back my car!"

The owl brought one of his wings to his beak and called out almost like a whistle, a hypersonic sound perceptible only to his hearing. The woman heard nothing except there was this strange sound from behind and rapidly approaching her.

There was something now pursuing her and the silhouette of a large butterfly shaded her from overhead from the sun, an enormous one, a butterfly perhaps 5000 times the size of an ordinary surface butterfly, almost as large as a Cessna airplane, rapidly descended.

Catching her from behind at the back of her knees, she bounced and then rolled across the back of the enormous creature as it rapidly flapped its wings.

They began to gain altitude with her now desperately grasping onto the head of the creature. Her body floated for a moment in midair and then settled on top of the butterfly's back.

She now was riding aboard this huge winged insect as they pursued the owl who was leading the way in the direction of a high hill that had been hidden by the trees.

Ahead, she now perceived there was an opening in the side of the hill, a large gaping hole, larger even than the butterfly she was now aboard.

It was more than a hole in the hillside; it was a massive tunnel whose entrance now closed behind all three. They were inside and the tunnel turned downward.

Downward, downward, downward, traveling faster than in an airplane in freefall descent, their speed ever accelerated, as they descended even further, literally through the planet, mile after mile, deeper than the deepest mine, deeper than the deepest of caves, the owl pursued by the butterfly with its sole passenger, continued their dive into the blackness beneath.

The woman temporarily became dizzy, disoriented from a strange colored gas she now smelled. Her surroundings around her began to spin out of control. She lost her grip on the butterfly's back and she fell from the insect and she began falling, falling, falling into the deepest, darkest of pits, deeper than was ever known.

She felt the rapid growth of two appendages sprouting out from her shoulder blades. The gas of the cave-tunnel was altering her biochemistry. She was now more than human. She was still in human form with butterfly wings, which were now maturing on her back, mimicking the last creature with which she had had physical contact.

Even though she had the wings of a butterfly, she still had not acquired the skill to properly use them in mid flight. Both the owl and the much larger butterfly immediately realized this.

The owl motioned to the butterfly and he complied by again accelerating, swooping beneath her as he had in the woods moments earlier, and breaking her fall.

All three continued their downward flight, deeper and deeper and still deeper within the earth. For miles and miles they traveled, nearly 4000 in all, nearing the center of the planet. The woman, who now had sprouted fully matured butterfly wings, appeared to be unconscious and the butterfly held onto her as they continued their descent to a warming light below.

It was an inner light — the light being given by a small, red, inner sun. As all three exited the passageway which had brought them from the surface of this world, they entered the hidden, subterranean and magical world of Montagua.

CHAPTER 4

MONTAGUA

She was confused and disoriented. Her world was no longer her own. Everything had been remade and reformed anew, for she retained no memory of who she had been on the surface world.

She had not been knocked unconscious by her collision on the back of a huge butterfly during her rapid, downward flight through the earth.

The gas in the subterranean passageway had acted much the same as that of a tranquilizer. She had merely fallen asleep.

The woman from above was awakening. And, her present appearance was far more youthful than it had been at sunrise earlier that day.

About the day — the day was no longer day, it was now soon to be nightfall. Nor was the sun now setting in the sky neither the same sun; nor was the moon the same moon.

It isn't every day that one falls for such a long of a time, if one would fall from such a great distance, from such a great height, that one would land from such a great fall without so much as having a broken bone, nor has any semblance of a marking, not even so much as having received even the tiniest of scratches, nor having any blemishes.

Her skin was unmarked. Her entire body lay absolutely supple and perfect.

Her eyelids fluttered for several moments. Her vision temporarily blurred in and out of focus, as if awakening from a very deep sleep.

The woman from above now found herself in an unknown land, surrounded by animals speaking to her in an unknown forest — the strangest of forests.

On the surface world, a forest was green and blue in color, but as she looked around these definitely were not the colors of this area she was lying prone on her back in. Everything looked much larger, overgrown, and gigantic in their proportions.

This particular, peculiar forest had the largest leaves, foliage of the strangest sizes and colors — oranges, reds, purples and blacks. Little did she realize the colors of how the earth was at its beginning when plant life first took hold?

One would also find that strange colors of foliage when illuminated by a red dwarf sun, radiating the red spectrum of light, unlike the surface's yellow sun, as was this hidden, subterranean world. It was foliage she had never recognized nor had ever seen in her life ever before.

She appeared to now possess very large wings, in exactly the same shapes and formations as those found on butterflies. She found she had control over these wings.

They were now attached to her on her back. She had full control over them. They moved as she willed them to move, to even the slightest attempt at movement of bending.

The wings had initially covered her like a blanket, but as she awoke they had unfolded into their full glory, pink and red near their centers, fully attached to her and now part of her anatomy. She moved them as freely as she could her arms and her legs.

All appendages, even the wings felt enormously strong. She picked up a small stone on the ground and crushed it into dust. She had such strength in her limbs and wings, as powerful as an insect's, if an insect were to grow to the size of a human being. Her new set of wings felt natural and normal to her. They were one with her and she was one with them.

Then, she had the most frightful experience as the heads of owls came into her view just above her. They had a look of most definite concern upon their faces for her well-being.

Furthermore, the owls were all speaking in her language, using words instead of uttering hoots and birdlike noises.

She observed several very large butterflies circling her from high overhead. Now that she had awakened, they had proceeded to land near her, as they took the most dainty and delicate of steps toward her.

These very large butterflies spoke no words. They uttered not a sound, but she could still understand that they were communicating with her in some strange way, as if telepathic in their nature. They spoke to her through formations of images in her mind — images that she could now understand, somehow, in some strange and unusual way.

She never could do this before in all the time she had been on the surface of this world. She was no longer human; she was now more than human.

She spread her wings and they brought her up from the ground in much the same way as arms would have pushed her upwards from her prone position. They were indeed attached to her and operated in exactly the same manner as did the other human appendages. The wings were now fully functional and most definitely part of her own anatomy.

She gazed up into what would have been the sky on the surface world. This sky was also blue, but it was a blue unlike any she had ever seen before, for this blue was the blue of ocean water, being illuminated by the light of a red, miniature setting sun.

The blue in the sky was seawater! It truly was seawater, with what now appeared to be a transparent dome between this subterranean cavern and the waters of the unknown ocean above.

Little did she realize that the glittering barrier between this hidden, inner world and the ocean above once consisted of a carbon substance once called coal. Coal, when placed under extreme pressure of the many miles of ocean waters above it for millions of years, eventually forms the hardest substance known — diamond!

The substance that was acting as a shield between this subterranean world and the miles and miles of waters above consisted of a purist form of diamond, completely transparent in this final state, which allowed her to see through the many miles of the ocean floor shielding all the way up through it, with only a slightly magnified visual distortion.

She wasn't sure if it was the Atlantic, or if it was the Pacific, or if it was the Arctic, or if it was any of the other four known oceans on the surface of the world.

She could now see sea life floating through miles of a protective transparent dome above her.

Strange aquatic life, but there was nothing so strange about this sort of sea life because she and the other creatures that surrounded her in this fully lighted subterranean cavern were no doubt miles beneath the surface of any ocean. The sea life was responding to the light of the internal sun, gathering their strengths and life-giving energies from it.

The soil beneath her feet, as she began to stand on them, was extremely soft and she sunk into the dirt. It was cool and its texture felt exactly like the same soil of her world on the surface where she had lived.

It was then, as she gazed down upon her bare feet half-covered in the soil on which she stood, that she also realized that her legs were bare, her entire torso was also so, as were her arms and wings. She bore no clothing upon her entire body.

"Oh my God," she whispered, "I have no clothing. I'm nude! I'm completely and totally naked!"

She quickly folded her legs and arms about herself and then, out of panic, she quickly began to run toward some nearby bushes in which to conceal her being naked.

During her run across the soft soil ground, her wings began to gather the warm breezes and she temporarily lifted off of the ground. She screamed in midair as she realized she was now airborne and tumbling uncontrollably in small, awkward half-somersaults, having not fully gained control of her new wings.

She soon swooped in larger circles, upward and downward, until finally losing complete control and splashing into a nearby shallow river she had drifted over. She was lying prone on her stomach in the middle of the waters and she pushed hard with her arms to bring herself up on her hands and knees.

It was then that she saw her reflection on the surface of the waters. She lifted one of her hands out of the water and gently touched her youthful face.

She was young again, younger than she had been in many, many years.

Her face was as young as that of a teenager, of perhaps 15 or 16 human years of age. Age was irrelevant here in this land. She remembered the giant owl stating there had never been any deaths in this land. She now was beginning to realize where she was.

She was in his land now. She was in Montagua.

Regardless of where she now knew she was, she was still lacking any sort of clothing. Her wings were now wet from the small stream of water she had landed in. For the moment, until they dried, she could not fly.

She stumbled to her feet and ran to the nearest set of bushes on the shoreline on the other side of the stream.

Back along the shore of the other side of the stream, one owl said to the owl who had discovered her on the surface, "Even with the butterfly wings, she still appears to be most human. Where did you find her, again?"

The owl who found her heavily sighed as he replied, "I found her on the surface world, just outside of the forest. I found her on the surface driving some sort of mechanical contraption."

"Ah. Humility. I should have guessed. It is a trait of their world. The Great Spirit should never have gifted humanity the characteristic of humility. It is the strangest of traits. It really does tend to get in the way of the natural order of things, at times."

"I quite agree, but I perceived she does have a great deal of potential for adding some much-needed excitement in this world. We could use some excitement down here. We haven't had her kind here in such a long time."

She began screaming, almost shrieking, from across the river behind the bushes, "What have you feathered vermin done with my clothing?"

The first owl said to the other beside him, "She does seem to be somewhat distraught, rather upset. Those garments we found her in were so confining. We thought we were doing her a favor by discarding them.

"Do we still have them? She still appears to be very human with a great desire to still have those items."

"Most human indeed," replied the other.

"Perhaps we should try to find them and comply with her wish to remain clothed? "I cannot imagine why? None of us wear strange outerwear."

She hollered at the top of her lungs again, this time using a series of far more vicious words.

"Oh, dear. Did you her use of forbidden words? Such language will never do. The Great Spirit will become most upset. He will banish her from here like he did to those other two humans so long ago."

"I don't think she fully realizes where exactly she is. No one has ever worn those outer garments that we found covering her here in Montagua. Perhaps you should try to calm her. Reassure her. There is no need for such strange garments here in this land."

More shrieks were heard from across the stream from the young woman with butterfly wings.

"She does seem rather insistent. I think it would be a good idea if we did gather them together for. You there, Number Two, she knows you better than she knows the rest of us. Those strange garments of hers will be found behind the bushes on the side of the stream.

"It appears as though she became so upset when she discovered that she was no longer wearing them, she didn't realize they were here nearby on our side of the stream. Please fly them over to her."

CHAPTER 5

FIRST FLIGHT

For the first few days, the girl with no name — for she couldn't remember her name — continued with the processes of learning her newfound abilities as a human-butterfly.

She learned the butterflies communicated with the flutter of their wings. And, here in Montagua, all butterflies were telepathic in nature. They had developed this ability over the thousands of years since Eden's conception.

She could hear and communicate all thoughts with every animal, with every creature, with every flower and with every blade of grass. Everything was alive. The foliage was strange in color, but its shapes were recognizable. Everything was red, orange or purple color. This had to do with the fact that there was an internal miniature red sun which illuminated the massive internal cavity in which Eden was encased.

She was especially fascinated with the ceiling of the cavern which consisted of diamonds, diamond of a transparent nature, through which she could see the waters of the seas above.

The Great Spirit had preserved his creation well when He had sunk this land below the waters above the dome using the waves of the great flood during Noah's time.

The owl who had found her, dazed and confused driving along that ancient back road and she became the very best of friends.

She named him "Hootie" because of his ceaseless chatter.

The owl always wanted to get the last word in — and usually did.

Hootie was instrumental in teaching her how to properly perform aerial manoeuvres and acrobatics with her new wings.

And, although she did not know her name, she was honestly becoming happy.

Her first flight over the waterway to retrieve her clothing from the other side had been clumsy, but she certainly was making great strides in learning how to use her winged appendages. They felt very natural and they were.

In the distance, at the far end of the cavern, there existed a great mountain. It was sacred, hallowed ground.

She was told by Hootie never go to the mountain. It was said that the Great Spirit lived there and watched over them and kept them safe and strife free. Hootie made her swear an oath, even though she could fly, to never try to reach the top of the mountain, for if she did, she would put them all in grave danger of the Great Spirit's wrath.

She was so fascinated by the diamonds in the sky — or rather what amounted to a sky. It was like living under a see-through aquarium. Miles and miles of seawater; the water obviously being the Ocean.

CHAPTER 6

AGEYUTSA

The girl with no name quickly became one with the Montagua community. Human beings were difficult on the surface world, but here, far beneath, in the land of Montagua, the human being had been sadly missed. The last known human being known to inhabit this hidden world was Archibald Crane, who had been missing after the final exploration that he took to the Great Mountain in the open Valley beyond.

The girl with no name was alone in that she did not have her own species for companionship, but she did not feel lonely, not in the least. She felt at peace.

For companionship, nearly every animal, except for the butterflies, which were insects, in truth. All animals spoke to her, they spoke in her language. They were able to interpret every human language on the planet, for they had lived through the entire lifespan of the planet. They had been around for thousands and thousands of years.

Her butterfly abilities gave her the capacity to communicate telepathically. So, when she wanted silence, she could still have conversation. She would simply flutter her wings at the appropriate frequencies.

The vibrations would be transmitted to the ears of the animals, plants or insects and be properly translated. All languages are really one language when spoken telepathically. All creatures are as one, as was intended by the Great Spirit, who is said to inhabit the far-off mountain in the distance.

Hootie had warned the girl with no name to never go on that mountain.

It was sacred, hallowed ground, long ago sanctioned by the ancient Indian tribes, long before Pangaea broke up into the seven known continents of today's world, long before the nomads and wanderers ventured forth over the land bridges, long before the first ice age.

It was believed that Montagua, according to an old book, with a black cover and gold lettering on its cover, was the first piece of land ever created by the Great Spirit.

It was pure and then untouched. The Great Spirit had hidden it from humanity because of that very fact.

Time did not exist in Montagua. Or, if it did, it progressed at a much, much lesser rate than it did on the surface of this world.

Even though 150 years had passed since Captain Crane had set foot on this land from above, after traveling by ship from the surface, he would've barely aged a day if even that. He could still very well be alive.

The girl with no name was tired of being called the girl with no name and Hootie understood this. He consulted with the tribal elders, the head of the owls and the leader of the Eagles.

It was decided by the head of the owls to bestow the name the ancient Cherokee word Ageyutsa for her name. Ageyutsa is the Cherokee word for girl — and it was certainly accurate. She was no doubt a girl, a girl with butterfly wings, but nevertheless a girl!

The girl graciously accepted being called Ageyutsa, but she was somewhat dismayed and disappointed when she learned of its uneventful meaning.

The leader of the owls explained to her that she was called Ageyutsa (or girl) because she had not really performed any great feats.

She was gifted with butterfly wings, she was swift, and very strong, of limb and of wing, and yet she had done very little in the land so far to prove her worth.

She would have to earn a new name. So, for now, Ageyutsa was very appropriate.

CHAPTER 7

ENCHANTRA'S REVENGE

Ageyutsa hated being called her assigned name, for the name meant only "girl" in Cherokee. The Cherokee people were one of the first Indian settlers in North America and they were extremely spiritual people.

So were the owls and the eagles in Montagua. All flying creatures in this underground land were very spiritual, no doubt influenced greatly by the Cherokee.

Hootie explained to Ageyutsa that the head of the owls, General Cornelius, had made an honest assessment of her, after consulting the Great Spirit who lived atop the far off High Mountain at the very center of the Land of Montagua.

She was new here. It was am honor to be named by the head of the owls. She would have to perform a simple duty of nightly patrols, by flight, over Montagua. It was an enormous task, due to Montagua's geographic size.

It was approximately, in square mileage, twice the size of the United States of America in the lower 49 states, excluding Alaska, from where she had entered.

Hootie was assigned to assist Ageyutsa in these nightly patrols over the land.

Hootie warned Ageyutsa never to go near a certain dwelling and female elf — her name was Enchantra, the sorceress, and her husband was Mordock, a most evil individual who could grow to gigantic proportions and sprout the blackest of wings.

He was a Nephilim, one of the ancient fallen angels, but Ageyutsa didn't realize what the term Nephilim meant.

Nor did she understand he was a fallen angel, only that he was an incredibly wicked man and that he was to be avoided, along with his wife.

Hootie never found this out, but, one daytime adventure that Ageyutsa decided to take without telling Hootie one afternoon, she decided to venture forth beyond the confines of the forest and she sought out this one called Enchantra on her own while Hootie was sleeping.

In her butterfly form, Ageyutsa decided to use her telepathic communication powers with the other insects to act as protection against this wicked one called Enchantra. She instructed several large swarms of bees to accompany her on this adventure.

When she finally located Enchantra, she had the bees dump several tons of their honey all over the sorceress. Enchantra became enraged and exceedingly jealous when she saw this winged creature, Ageyutsa, flying over her head and out of her immediate reach.

She would have gouged out Ageyutsa's eyes out with her long fingernails had she had the chance. Enchantra believed that her husband, Mordock to be the only one capable of flight who had human form.

Ageyutsa impishly decided to play a practical joke on the sorceress. With the swarms of bees now under her control, Ageyutsa instructed them to position themselves in an attack formation after dumping all of their honey all over Enchantra.

Upon doing this, the sorceress shook her fist violently in the air at Ageyutsa and swore revenge, warning her that she would tell Mordock, her husband, the giant.

These were not just idle threats voiced by Enchantra, she was most serious with her threat, and she would follow through.

That evening, Ageyutsa made no mention of her mischievous adventure to Hootie. It would be a secret that would later come back to haunt her, in a most serious and world-threatening way, for one should never enrage the wife of a fallen archangel.

Hootie and Ageyutsa became a team and they became the closest of companions, spending each day in the forest, surrounded by all this beauty. They told stories to each other of both worlds by a campfire each night.

Hootie told Ageyutsa of a branch of the Cherokee tribe that ventured underground, coming into contact with those in Montagua many centuries ago.

Indeed, Ageyutsa soon learned it was the Cherokee people who had renamed this underground world Montagua from its original name.

She asked Hootie what the original name of this place was. He could not remember, exactly. But he remembered it being mentioned in an old book, an artifact left behind by a certain Captain Archibald Crane in a mighty ship.

The name Archibald Crane caught her attention. She remembered going to the Captain's notes before climbing the mountain in Alaska.

She could not still remember her name, but she did remember the events leading up to her memory loss. It was the strangest thing. She could remember those details with much clarity, but she still could not remember her own name.

Hootie explained to her that there was an old book left behind by Captain Crane on a wooden podium at the base of the great mountain. He would take her to it.

It was a long shot, but perhaps reading through those old notes left by Captain Crane would help her remember her own name in a very indirect way, as she did describe in detail much of her research on the good Captain and his crew aboard *The*

Venture, about how they got lost seeking an underground world much like this one nearly 150 years earlier.

The next day, Hootie flew with Ageyutsa to the foot of the great mountain. Foliage had grown over the podium over its many years of standing in isolation, but Ageyutsa soon uncovered the old book which turns out to be an early Gutenberg Bible left behind by Captain Archibald Crane.

The two adventurous companions began reading as they opened the book. It was a Bible. The ancient Bible contained drawings, and hand illustrations left behind by Crane.

Ageyutsa began to recognize the area from the illustrations and soon realized that the drawings in the book, the pictures in particular, exactly matched the surrounding area, including the mountain on which the Great Spirit was said to exist.

They were at the foot of that very mountain at this moment.

It was Ageyutsa who came to a startling conclusion. She knew what she was now. The pieces began to fit together — no human beings, all animals and insects. Nothing ever aged. Everything was young and new. Everything was always renewing itself. And then there was this photograph of the mountain in the book which matched exactly.

The location had not changed in over 500 years. It was exactly the same.

"Hootie, the old name of this place that you cannot remember – I know where we are now.

"Why didn't this come to me before? Captain Crane was looking for Eden, the place where the Garden of Eden was known to exist.

"Hootie, Captain Crane discovered what he was looking for.

"He found the Garden of Eden! It has been here all along. It has been down here, probably since Noah's flood. All that water must've pushed the entire landmass down through the cave systems you brought me through to get here, into this massive underground cavern!

"Hootie, we are in the Garden of Eden! The Great Spirit — my God!

"Could the Great Spirit be God himself?

"Hootie, please, tell me everything you know about this Great Spirit. I must know. I NEED to know. My mouth has gone dry from the excitement, I — I — I need a drink of water."

She began looking around.

"Or perhaps even something stronger! That's stream over there. It has a crimson color, almost like wine. The Great Spirit, the Lord, was capable of turning water into wine. I wonder if it is possible. Could that be wine? Hootie, I have to taste it to find out!

"You stay here — or are you coming with me? Either way, we'll find out together. C'mon! Let's fly over there — now!"

Both Hootie and Ageyutsa fly over to the distant stream. It was indeed flowing red. It looked like wine, but Hootie began to realize that something was definitely wrong.

He began warning her, "Ageyutsa, don't drink —!" But it was already too late. Ageyutsa had cupped her hands and had brought the liquid to her face. She had already begun consuming it. It was like drinking fire. She screamed in agony, her features darkening, and fangs began to roll from the sides of her mouth. This was black magic. Hootie realize this was the typical work of Enchantra. She had poisoned the water with one of her black magic spells. And now, Ageyutsa was the victim.

Hootie looked at the water and then at her. She was gasping heavily and began to look up at the ceiling of the cavern. She growled under her breath, "I need blood. Human blood. I have this uncontrollable urge. I have this thirst. It must be quenched. The humans are above. I must —!"

Hootie ran to his female companion, whom he could barely recognize at this point as being Ageyutsa. She was a human-butterfly.

One of the attributes of being a butterfly, at certain particular times of the year, was that they thirsted for human blood. Enchantra had caused this genetic feature to emerge in Ageyutsa.

Ageyutsa was still half human and far stronger than a butterfly. Her urges would be that much stronger. It would be practically uncontrollable. In her current state, Ageyutsa was much like a vampire. And as strong as one.

Hootie had to risk his life. He had to somehow stop her, before she could take flight. She was probably strong enough in her current condition to slice through the diamond ceiling of the cavern and bore her way all the way to the surface of the earth.

With her current strengths and with her ability to fly and with her size, she would be practically unstoppable except by a small army.

He could think of only one thing to do. He had to allow her to touch him — to come into physical contact with him.

He had avoided doing this in the past because there was every chance that she would acquire his strength, his abilities and his traits of the now. But amplified that strength of 1000 times over, just like the butterfly, she would become 1000 times stronger than any owl of the planet.

She would become swift, as fast as a jet fighter, given her human size and she would also retain her butterfly capabilities from her previous contact as well. Hootie knew all of this and yet he risked it all.

Ageyutsa was practically going insane trying to control herself at this point. There were so many urges welling up inside of her from Enchantra's poison water.

This was black magic for sure — and she had to become an owl. She could not remain in her butterfly form much longer or she would lose her sanity and complete control of her mind.

Hootie said, grabbing hold of her with both wings, "Ageyutsa! Ageyutsa! Listen to me, Ageyutsa! Let your human half still hear me. You are experiencing black magic and it is affecting your butterfly portions of your personality.

"You must become an owl to overcome them. You must become another hybrid creature. If you become an owl, you will not have the urge for human blood.

"Hear me, Ageyutsa! Listen to what I'm telling you! All you have to do is touch my left or right wing.

"Either one, and the urge will go away. You will become a human-owl! Your abilities will greatly increase, but the urge to drink blood will be gone from you! Owls have no desire to drink blood. Only butterflies, but not owls. You must become a human-owl!

"Bear but a touch of my wing, Ageyutsa! Ageyutsa, hold yourself steady and touch my wing! You cannot continue like this! It will drive you insane. Don't let Enchantra's magic trick you like this. Don't let her win! Become an owl. Become a human-owl! All you have to do is touch my wing. That's all you have to do and the urges will go away"

Ageyutsa kept looking at the ceiling of the cavern, but then, she kept looking away from it shaking her head, trying to clear it. She finally obeyed Hootie and touched his right wing. She began to transform.

Her face was half owl – half human. The transformation was nearly complete. She held Hootie tightly to herself. Their hearts beat as one. Her eyesight greatly improved as did her reflexes. Her wings began to alter themselves. Black blotches temporarily grew out of half of her face. Owl feathers began to form. Butterflies could not speak, but owls always could.

She began chirping like an owl.

The uncontrollable urges to drink human blood subsided. She was over twice the size of Hootie, but she was a human-owl. She held onto Hootie and lifted him off the ground, kissing him for what he had done, for showing such bravery. The fangs were gone. The vampire urge to drink blood had been removed from her through the transformation to an owl. Ageyutsa once again began to think and breathe normally once more.

CHAPTER 8

CAPTAIN ARCHIBALD CRANE AND THE HMS VENTURE

Over the next week, Ageyutsa practiced transforming from being a butterfly-human to an owl-human repeatedly until she had mastered the technique.

Fortunately, most of her human body remained human in appearance, even after such transformations.

But there were definite benefits to being an owl over being a butterfly.

Her range of flight was greatly improved.

Ageyutsa soon discovered that her flight capabilities had been greatly enhanced from being a butterfly-human when she had transformed into an owl-human.

Owls have the ability to fly silently — like a jet in stealth mode. They are able to swoop low and almost hover like a helicopter, with very little movement required from their wings.

Ageyutsa, being over twice the size of a large owl, had these abilities greatly augmented.

Her maximum speed of flight had also been greatly improved. She was not tossed around by heavy winds.

Each of her five senses, chiefly, her hearing and eyesight had dramatically improved.

She was now a creature of the night, with the strength and power of a predator.

She still retained the ability to communicate with all creatures through the flutter of her wings that she had had while being a butterfly-human, but now she was able to perform aerial manoeuvres far superior to that of a butterfly as an owl-like creature of the night. She could now easily keep up with Hootie. In fact, since her wings were much larger than Hootie's, she was far faster.

Her strength — her natural strength — had increased by a factor of 20. She could uproot almost any tree, if she chose to do so. But she tried to limit her great strength and still have a gentle touch.

She immediately noticed and was extremely grateful that she no longer had a craving for human blood.

Enchantra's potion had been nullified when Ageyutsa had made her first transformation into an owl-human after touching Hootie's wing at the foot of the mountain, by the edge of the mighty stream.

Hootie and Ageyutsa extended their patrolling range far beyond the forest.

Much further down the cavern, there existed a body of water almost as large as Lake Superior. The large lake let out into both the Atlantic and the Pacific oceans upon splitting apart much further downstream.

It was on their very first patrol over the large lake that they saw a large sailing vessel. It was *The Venture*. Ageyutsa absolutely recognized this ship from her memory of reading through the old book at the foot of the mountain. It was part of the notes which Captain Crane had left behind:

An old Daguerreotype photograph and interior design of his exploratory vessel commissioned to him by Queen Victoria in the year 1875.

Indeed, although the ship had disappeared nearly 150 years ago, it still looked brand-new out of dry dock.

The ship had not aged.

There was no sign of wear, no water damage, no barnacle buildup, it was remarkable. Then again, they were in the land of Eden, a land that was not subject to the ravages of time.

But, what about the crew? Could they possibly be alive? Who was steering the ship? Was it an old derelict, a ghost ship? Had the ship been abandoned?

All of these questions whirled through Ageyutsa's mind as both she and Hootie swooped low, nearly touching the waves they swung along *The Venture*'s Stern.

They had been noticed! For who would not notice a flying woman sprouting very large, feathered owl wings being accompanied by still another very large owl?

Even though Ageyutsa tried to whisper to Hootie, her voice was carrying over the water and so was Hootie's responses to her.

This shocked the Captain — a flying owl-woman being accompanied by a talking owl!

Captain Crane motioned to his crew to remain calm until their intentions were truly known. Where they friend? Or were they foe?

Long ago, Captain Crane adventured on land and through the great jungles and forests to discover the Eternity Mountain, where he had left the Gutenberg Bible and other notes on a podium at its base.

He had built the podium out of wood in the area. The Bible he carried with him, along with his notes from his diary in a sack on his back.

He had met no animals, no birds, and certainly nothing human on that trip inland so long ago.

The Captain's watch had stopped. It had stopped not because it was broken, but because there was no passage of time in this great under-land and undersea cavern of which Eden was a part.

"Hold! Who are you? You, and your owl that lands on my deck, state your purpose — are you friend or foe?

"Is this not America? You, woman, you certainly look American! And you spoke over the water — your accent was most assuredly American.

"Did the President send you? On behalf of her Majesty Queen Victoria, I bid you welcome, if you are sent by your president.

"But, be warned, if your intention is to distract or disrupt any of my crew or any of the ship's operation, you will be taken below and put in irons.

"State who sends you. State your purpose. State whom you are! And state your intention, now! Not a step further. Speak."

Ageyutsa knew that her hearing had vastly improved, but still, she had to ask, "Are you Captain Crane? And, did you just mention Queen Victoria?"

"Aye to both of your questions, ma'am. I have never seen one such as you. Who or what are you?"

"I am — I am — let's just say, I'm a human being, with advanced capabilities. The actual explanation is far too long and complex to accept or explain.

"Do you still believe this Queen Victoria's time? You said I'm an American. I am, Captain. You are correct.

"But, if I might ask, whom do you believe the president to be? What year do you think this is?"

"The answer to your second question is the easy one. It is the year 1875, is it not? Or, perhaps we were at sea for quite a while. It could quite likely be 1876?

"It is your centennial year then, if it is so. Is that why the president dispatched you to greet us? Are you celebrating your centennial anniversary here in America?"

"You believe this to be our centennial? It is true you are in America — technically under America, but as to the year — well —! You're in for a bit of a shock. Just whom do you believe the president is at this time?"

"Let me think for a moment, my good woman… Why, your president is —Ulysses S Grant, ma'am."

"Ulysses S?!? — No. No, Captain. I'm afraid not. Brace yourself. What I have to tell you it's hard to believe. Just as difficult as it is to believe that these wings I have are the wings of an owl, but they are.

"Captain, listen to me very carefully — you and your crew have been caught up in what is known as a time warp.

"That is what you passed through from the surface to get here.

"Captain, I believe it was called the chronometer in your time. What was your last chronometer reading?"

"This ship's chronometer stopped working a long time ago."

"A very long time ago, Captain Crane.

"Captain Crane, prepare yourself for a shock. Steady yourself, now.

"Welcome to the 21st century. Welcome to the year 2023.

"You, your crew and your ship have been trapped inside this 6000-mile subsurface cavern for nearly 150 years.

"Captain, you set out to find Eden. You have done that, Sir. You will likely be promoted to the rank of admiral, for your efforts, assuming you can ever find a way to leave.

"And, from what you've just told me, the likelihood of that happening is extremely remote.

"If you haven't found a route by now, there likely isn't one. I'm afraid you're trapped here, just like every other living thing down here.

"Not to worry, though. All creatures live forever. You have the rest of forever to figure out a way to get back to the surface world.

"I am afraid you are trapped here, just like every other creature here in the Garden of Eden. If there is a way, only God himself knows it."

CHAPTER 9

MORDOCK, THE SORCERER

Genesis 6:4 reads as follows: "Nephilim were in the earth in those days, and also after that, when the sons of God came in unto the daughters of men, and they bore children to them; the same were the mighty men that were of old, the men of renown."

With Ageyutsa, Hootie, and all manner of animal in the Land of Montagua defeating the gnome invasion from beneath the earth, peace was temporarily restored upon the planet.

But, there remained one who remained undefeated under or upon the earth. There existed one called Mordock, the Sorcerer. He was one without age, and most ancient. He was one of the mighty men that were of old, men of renown.

He was a giant who could reduce himself to the size of an ordinary man, and conceal his dark and blackened wings.

He was the last generation of the Nephilim.

He was one of the original fallen Angels. He was an Archangel; he was the son of Lucifer.

CHAPTER 10

TO TOUCH THE SKY

With Ageyutsa still being half human, she can no longer resist the urge to fly upward to the diamond ceiling of the inner cavern containing Eden; she begins to climb the Great Mountain in the center of the Valley of Eden, where the Great Spirit is said to live.

She begins her accent in her owl-form, but soon realizes that she is in her owl form limited and cannot reach the peak of the mountain to touch the diamond sky still several thousand feet above her.

She then notices some Eagles flying high above her and she launches herself upward from the side of the mountain on which she is perched, briefly coming in contact with one of the Eagles in flight.

Ageyutsa undergoes a third transformation from being half owl/half human to being half Eagle/half human, acquiring the abilities of Eagles while still retaining the old characteristics of being an owl, as well as her former form of being part butterfly.

Finally, enthralled by the glittering of the diamonds encrusted in the ceiling of the cavern, in her Eagle form, Ageyutsa gets to touch the diamond ceiling that encapsulates Montagua.

Ageyutsa is distracted by a disturbing sound below as she sees legions of owls hastily retreating from where the four rivers cross in the land of Eden.

There is a giant figure emerging from the waters and the owls are fleeing in fear. Mordock, a fallen archangel, the son of Lucifer, has grown to over 100 feet in height and with a menacing stare has frightened many of the animals, including the owls, as their armies retreat. Just as Lucifer had control over all creatures on the earth, so too does the son of Lucifer possess such control.

His arms were raised high in the air and Ageyutsa now realizes the entirety of the land of Eden is traveling upward through the waters of the oceans.

Eden is resurfacing, pushing upward through the mantel's seismic plates under the United States of America producing a thousand-mile-long super volcano at its dead center as the tectonic plates on and under the North American Continent begin to bulge and split apart from the upward black magical pressures being exerted from a fallen archangel standing on the shores of the submerged sub continent underneath.

On the West Coast, the San Andreas Fault line has been fully activated; California and the state of Washington are slowly falling into the Pacific Ocean.

Out on the East Coast, New York City is now half underwater, the Statue of Liberty collapsing in New York Harbor, the city begins to slip into the Atlantic, along with Boston and all major cities along the coastline, including the entire states of Florida and Georgia, once nearly at sea level, they are now being submerged.

The subterranean continent of Eden, twice the size of the United States is now being thrust upward from the fallen archangel Mordock's black magic incantations.

"Arise, O Eden! Let the world feel my wrath! The time for Armageddon upon the earth has come. Let America shake and quiver at my power, for I shall be their new ruler. Indeed, this entire world is nothing but my toy — mine did choose whether to play with or to destroy, at my leisure and at my will!

"O, my Father Lucifer, give me the strength I need to raise this land above America, for thine is the kingdom and the power and the glory, in thy name, I do this for thee!"

Ageyutsa, in her Eagle form, was nearly half the height of Mordock is at his present giant size and she rapidly descends from the rising ceiling, downward in an attack posture.

Realizing the Giants often have limited vision, Ageyutsa attempted to attack Mordock from the side. Now, most of the waters, after incredible speed is been gained through her dive from high atop the cavern, Ageyutsa alters her trajectory upward and bringing both fists together to form a hammer-like blow, she strikes the giant Mordock directly in the jaw, knocking the enormous figure off his feet momentarily he falls backward on his backside on the shoreline. He shook his head to clear the cobwebs from Ageyutsa's blow, as Ageyutsa has felt the shock wave from the strike all the way up into her shoulders. It was like striking rock, not flesh. It was like moving a mountain and, although Ageyutsa has greatly increased her strength in her Eagle form, she soon realizes that Mordock is far more than mortal.

The giant soon recovers and is once again on his feet, this time taking a far more solid stance he becomes immovable, utilizing his high density as an Archangel. Ageyutsa, although she strikes him several times more, these blows are becoming less and less effective in her efforts to strike down the giant.

Hootie, watching the battle, exclaims "He flies, just like Ageyutsa and me. He is a fallen one! An Archangel! Ageyutsa, you can't win! Stop, before he kills you!"

His wings were as dark as a raven's. His body shaped as a Greek God and as hardened steel. He transfigured and transformed right before Ageyutsa into a dragon.

Ageyutsa fought with him, but he was too strong for even her in her Eagle form.

He swats Ageyutsa to the other shoreline where she crashes heavily on the ground beside Hootie who was witnessing this heroic fight between the giant Eagle Ageyutsa and the Archangel Mordock.

"Ageyutsa! Ageyutsa, he is too strong! Stay down! You are no match for him even in your present Eagle form. That is an Archangel. That is a spiritual being. He is simply too powerful for you to overcome! We have to call in the cavalry, I will try to get help from the surface — call in the Army, the Navy — Nuke him out of existence! His strength is not natural. His strength is that of Lucifer, his father!"

"Hootie, you don't understand, I am the cavalry. These simple woods' animals cannot possibly defend themselves against a monster like that. I'm the only chance we have. He is trying to change the course of the four rivers that flow into this cavern. If he succeeds, everything will dry up, wither away and die!

"I will try to detain him long enough for you to bring help, but please hurry. He is so strong! And his flesh is like rock. Hitting him is like striking a volcano!"

"So, you are the legendary Ageyutsa and is now a mighty magical eagle," but then he said, "I know all about magic, for I am all about magic!"

And he lashed out and struck her.

He struck her in midflight so hard the earth shook for miles around. Everything began to grow dark during their battle. Lightning came crashing down from the sky above us as they fought.

It was black magic that he used against her. Hootie saw what he did.

Mordock reached down into the grass in the woods and withdrew a 50 foot python which lay hidden. Using a magical incantation, the snake hardened and went rigid in the form of an arrow. He had formed a living arrow from a snake, a python!

He brought the snake-arrow near her face, as Ageyutsa struggled within his grasp allowing her head to be transformed to that of an eagle she bit him hard with her beak, drawing blood from him.

Ageyutsa somehow manages to free herself momentarily from his tightening grasp.

"No matter how high you fly, Ageyutsa, let's see if you can out run this! Mighty Python, find thy target!"

She began to fly away, but then he withdrew the bow from his back and shot her with the python-arrow, which struck her left wing.

Ageyutsa screams in pain, her left wing now useless and going numb, she begins to drop from the sky. It is Hootie who rescues her, catching her under her wounded wing, keeping her aloft as he flew tight to her side, supporting her, not allowing her to crash upon the ground, they soar into the air once more, together, each supporting the other.

Hootie looked ahead and saw the mountain of eternity at the very center of Eden. He knew the Great Spirit was said to live there. Ageyutsa was being overtaken by the poison, she was losing consciousness. Finding the Great Spirit on Eternity Mountain was now Ageyutsa's, Hootie's and all of Eden's only hope for survival against the onslaught of the giant Archangel Mordock.

Hootie, carrying Ageyutsa in the air had barely enough lift in his own wings to reach the top of the mountain where both he and Ageyutsa fell heavily — fortunately — into the newly fallen snow high up on the mountaintop.

"Hootie," whispered Ageyutsa, "I just cannot go any further. I am going to die here on this mountaintop. I — I — cannot —"

Ageyutsa had passed out from the poisonous snake-arrow still embedded, impaling her left wing.

CHAPTER 11

HE WHO WALKS AMONG US

The man with the hood — or what appeared to be just a man — gently lifted the wounded Ageyutsa under the watchful eye of Hootie.

The owl began explaining what had happened, but the man already understood, as if he'd already had knowledge of what had transpired far below the mountain. He lifted a finger to his lips in a gesture for silence.

The hooded man finally spoke.

"She has been struck by an arrow and it appears her wound on her left wing bears the marks of being bitten by a snake in the garden. This arrow looks like it is of the form of a snake.

"So, it is clear. Mordock clearly is upon the earth."

"Ageyutsa. Her name is Ageyutsa. I met her on the surface of this world and she has become a mighty warrior here in Montagua, but she was no match for this sorcerer."

Hootie continued to tell the stranger every detail, almost in a blind panic as he spoke, "He flew, just like Ageyutsa and me. He was a sorcerer.

"His wings were as dark as a raven's. His body shaped as a Greek God and as hardened steel. He transfigured and transformed right before us into a dragon.

"Ageyutsa fought with him, but he was too strong for even her in her eagle form.

"He said, she was a mighty magical eagle, but then he said, I know all about magic, for I am all about magic, and he lashed out and struck her.

"He struck her so hard the earth shook for miles around us. I felt it. Everything grew darkened during their battle. Lightning came crashing down from the sky above us as they fought.

"It was black magic that he used against her. I saw what he did. He formed an arrow from a snake, a python!

"He brought the snake-arrow near her face.

"Ageyutsa somehow managed to free herself momentarily from his grasp. She began to fly away, but then he shot her with the arrow.

"I saw this mountain far off in the distance. I assisted Ageyutsa to fly one more time by supporting her under her wounded wing for as long as she could, but she fainted in the sky and we both fell to the earth.

"Still, together we flew here for sanctuary. I know this is sacred ground.

"It is against the ancient Eden laws to come here. This is where the first human transgression took place, many millennia ago. I know that. And the Great Spirit is said to exist here. I know all of that, also.

"But I had to bring her here to get her to safety, away from that wicked sorcerer living at the foot of the mountain."

The stranger spoke, "I know of this sorcerer. His name is Mordock. Mordock is an immortal — an Archangel — or rather the son of an Archangel. He was born over a millennium ago during the reign of King Arthur.

"He defied King Arthur and he was banished. He obviously has found his way to Eden over the centuries. Only one such as Mordock is capable of such treachery.

"Mordock is the son of another Archangel, the most powerful Archangel of all time, an Archangel once going by the name of Lucifer.

"So, Hootie, it is all coming together for me now. The reason why I was told to return by my Father. It was Mordock who did this to her."

"You know my name."

"I know all names. I know of all names of every man, woman and creature upon this earth and under it," the hooded stranger replied.

"There are rumors — more of a legend than a rumor — that the Great Spirit lives in this region of the mountain. Are you he? Are you the Great Spirit?" asked Hootie.

"That's not what's important right now, my gentle friend. You did well by bringing her here. We must tend to your friend. Let's get Ageyutsa out of this cold, into some place warm. The cave ahead will serve. I have blankets and a small supply of food and water within it."

"Is she going to die? The wound looks bad."

"She will not die. But we must remove the arrow and then remove his poison from her. She must become as strong as an Archangel — as strong as Mordock. Only then, can she survive. She will live, Hootie. I promise you.

"But you must not reveal what I am about to do to help her. You must not reveal this to anyone, Hootie. Do you understand me?"

"Whoooo are you?" he asked, his head bellowing upward, as he gazed into the man's eyes.

"Who I am, right now, is of no importance."

"Are you Captain Archibald Crane? She was looking for —"

"No. I am not Captain Crane. If I revealed who I am, all that I am, in truth, you would not believe me, nor would she."

"She does not seem to be responding."

"She is unconscious. She has lost a lot of blood. It is just as well that she does not hear this conversation.

"Come. Let us go forth. The cave is ahead. We must remove her footwear, for the ground ahead is hallowed ground. It is sacred. Do you understand that, Hootie?"

"Is it an ancient Indian burial place?"

"No. It is sacred because I am here. I have returned."

"You speak in riddles. Whooo are you?"

"I have already explained to you — if I revealed who I am, all that I am, your mind couldn't take it. All I ask is that you have faith in me that I can heal your friend. Come. Let us go. We need to get Ageyutsa out of this cold."

"You know her name?"

"I've already told you I know all names — of every living creature, of every star in the sky. My Father has named each one of them and all of us."

"Whoooo in the hell are you?" spat out Hootie, now irritated with all this runaround talk. Who was this man? And he kept his face hidden from view, well cloaked beneath that hood he had on.

The man simply smiled at him and said, "I should not tolerate that language, but under the circumstances, I shall. Let us go.

"Your friend, Ageyutsa, has the ability to acquire the traits of any creature she comes in contact with. I am aware of this. We shall use it to her advantage. She must become as strong as an Archangel. She must become the very first female Archangel. Only I can make this so."

"You are a crazy, old hermit. That's what you are! You're absolutely crazy if you think you can —!"

"Stay Calm and come with me, my owl friend. We have no time to waste — and I must do what I must do in order for Ageyutsa to survive. And, Mordock is now among us. Time grows short."

Inside the cavern, the stranger carried Ageyutsa as Hootie flew along beside them. There was a bed, more like an elaborate cot, in the innermost chamber of the cavern. The stranger gently lay Ageyutsa upon the bedding.

His hand gently touched the wounded area on her left wing. A brilliant light began emanating from the damaged region and the arrow was removed from her without feeling the slightest pain. Upon the arrow's removal, it immediately turned into a venomous snake.

Hootie gasped, but the stranger told him it was an ancient Egyptian trick performed by magicians. He told the owl he had nothing to fear. Both he and Ageyutsa were safe in his presence and he heightened his voice and simply spoke the words, "Be gone, old wicked serpent!"

The snake curling and coiling along on the floor was engulfed in a white light and soon vanished from existence.

The stranger turned his attention back to Ageyutsa. She was trembling. She had been severely poisoned and it was coursing through every vein of her body. The stranger began to comfort and he removed his hood, revealing his true identity.

Ageyutsa's and Hootie's eyes widened in disbelief.

The stranger spoke directly to Ageyutsa, "Ageyutsa, I am the Lord thy God. I have returned. Do you believe in me or not?"

"You — you cannot possibly be here! It is impossible! I must be hallucinating!"

"Ageyutsa," he paused and spoke in a far more gentle voice, "Ageyutsa, faith overrides the impossible. It always has. And it always will.

"To conquer death, I only had to die. I was nailed to a cross over 2000 years ago and I died on that cross, for you and for everyone on this planet and for everyone on other planets throughout the entire universe.

"I am the Lord thy God. Thou shalt not perish! Believe in me — now — and you will not see death, not here, not now, but I am going to prove to you the absolute power of my Father in heaven.

"Now, at this very moment, He and I and the Holy Spirit are going to alter history in a very slight but most significant way. Take my hand. You see on my hand the scars of the crucifixion that I endured over two of your millennia ago.

"Your soul shall become one with my soul. I long ago lived as a man, a human being, in this world. Your life shall become mine and mine shall become yours.

"You are about to be reborn as the very first female Archangel. A species that has never existed, but my Father in heaven has made this decision for you.

"As a new species of Archangel, you shall have full command over all of the physical laws of the universe, as does every other Archangel that has ever existed.

"There is a poison traveling through your body. As an Archangel, seek it out at the molecular level and change its chemistry into that of your own blood. You can do this — as a female Archangel you will have such power, but to become an Archangel, you must allow your soul to be merged with my own. Do you understand?"

"My Lord, I am afraid. I do not fully understand what you say."

"You need not understand, simply have faith in Me. I am the Christ. I am the son of God. Through Me and through my Father, all things are possible. Do you believe in Me or not?"

"I feel your hand. I feel the warmth of your hand holding mine and I am comforted in a way that I have never been comforted. I am a thief, Lord. I am not worthy."

"I, the Lord Jesus Christ of Nazareth, the son of Joseph and Mary, born into this world many, many years ago, say that you are worthy in my eyes.

"Prepare yourself, Ageyutsa. You are about to relive my first life on this earth, so that you will fully understand and remove any fear you might have. Remember, always, Ageyutsa, through Me, your Lord, all things are possible. Only believe. Only believe. Now shut your eyes — and when you reawaken, I will be with you.

Ageyutsa's body gave up the ghost, but, as the Lord had promised, she did not die. Her eyes opened once more and she found herself lying in the manger in a little town called Bethlehem, over 2000 years earlier.

Ageyutsa and Jesus now shared the same body, with their souls together.

For the 33 years of Jesus' life, Ageyutsa also experience that very same life — every moment, every feeling, every pain, every sorrow, every joy and every moment with the Lord as he grew from baby, to a child, to a fully grown man, but more than a man — far more than a man, for he was the son of the Almighty God.

The Lord had mentioned that both He and the Father and the Holy Ghost had decided to alter history in a very slight way.

And, although she experienced Jesus' crucifixion on that cross at Calvary, Jesus' last words were now, "Father, into Thy hands WE COMMIT OUR SPIRITS."

Over 2000 years later, the lifeless body of Ageyutsa shot upright in bed. She was seeing and hearing everything on the face of the earth — every sound, every voice, human and nonhuman, every plant, every animal, every car horn blaring, every blade of grass growing, every whistle sounding, every sound found in nature, every noise made by man and by woman, all 7.8 billion people on the planet, every animal, every bird in the sky, the flutter of their wings, every butterfly flying.

She was seeing everything, all images, from smallest to the largest, and all at once. She was no longer human, nor butterfly, nor owl, nor eagle. She was spiritual. She had become a spirit. In a spirit form she encircled the globe.

Her form had changed from that of an eagle-human.

She no longer sprouted eagle's wings, but fully developed wings of an Archangel. The very first female Archangel, Ageyutsa, drew her first breath upon the earth.

As the Lord had promised, she did not die. She had conquered death and had become immortal.

Her heart was still human, but the rest of her was spirit, pure spirit, and any doubts she may have had about that man who had been holding her hand, which she now perceived to be only moments ago, had been erased; he truly was the Lord thy God, Jesus Christ, born on to the Virgin Mary and to the carpenter Joseph over 2000 years ago, for she had lived and had experienced every moment of his own life in conjunction with her own.

CHAPTER 12

CHARLIE, THE DISGRUNTLED CHERUB

The Lord told Ageyutsa to rise from the bed. He began explaining to her that she was now a new species. She was no longer human, nor animal, nor an insect nor any combination of the three. She was now an Archangel, but still possessing a human heart. The Lord had refused to alter that particular trait, for it would become her greatest strength, but also her greatest weakness, unless she was very, very careful. He warned her, both his Father and He held Archangels to a much higher standard than human beings.

He expected perfection as an end product, but he would be merciful and understanding and compassionate to her new position, but only to a point.

She would have to prove herself through angelic training, much like going to boot camp, before becoming a lieutenant in the Army of God. She was a female angel, and an Archangel, she was in God's Army now. She needed training.

The Lord also knew that Mordock, the son of Lucifer, was now upon the earth and he had to seek him out, discover his whereabouts, and contain him before permanent, irreparable damage could be done to Eden, the planet Earth and to all of human kind.

He, therefore, decided not to train his new Archangel, this female Archangel. He had a dual purpose in mind.

His name was Charlie. Charlie was a cherub. There are nine ranks among the Angels. Cherubs are of a higher ranking than Archangels, because they are, supposedly — I say supposedly — closer to God.

This was especially true of Charlie. Charlie had been disenchanted. He had become disgruntled. In the Lord's words, as he described him to Ageyutsa, he needed to be "Re-gruntled".

Charlie had held protests against the Lord in heaven, stating that he was too bias — that all Angels were male Angels and he was sick of it, sick to death of it!

As a matter of fact, there was no gender associated with Angels, up until the creation of Ageyutsa, the very first female Archangel.

So, the Lord, in all his infinite wisdom, had finally decided to put Charlie's suggestion to the test. And thus was created the very first female Archangel in the form of Ageyutsa.

Ageyutsa, of course, fully agreed and complied with the Lord's wishes, but Charlie would be another matter altogether.

Charlie would be a bit of a hard-sell.

The Lord called out to Charlie, "Charlie? Charlie!"

There was no answer.

The Lord called out again, "Charlie, this is the Lord Jesus Christ, I need thee to appear before me.

"Charlie, I command of thee for the second time — Charlie, appear before me this instant. Thus sayeth the Lord!"

This time, there was a response, a response that could be heard echoing through the air, "I'm taking a wizz."

"He can't be serious. He's not human. He doesn't have to abide by —" "Be with you in a moment, Jesus. I'm doin' my duty. Nature is callin'. "Now, You knows even I must abide by nature, Lord. Especially after you disenchanted me.

"Practically turned me into one of those blasted humans."

"See what I mean by disgruntled?" questioned the Lord to Ageyutsa, "he's downright spiteful!

"No more words like blasted from you! There's a lady present down here. You mind your manners."

"Ladies is still only human beings. I'm a cherub. I'll say what a damned well want to do — because I am damned. You know how hard it is to hit the toilet? Or what amounts to be a toilet up here?

"Especially, since I ain' t been human in over 300 years. I'm kind of out of practice."

"Charlie, hurry up. And don't forget to clean yourself up using holy water. Make yourself presentable. I've got someone special to show you. Something even you haven't seen — and Archangel! The special kind of Archangel you've been —"

"I've been around the archangels. There ain't nothing special about any of them. They just think they's special.

"Why, I can tell you about the time that —!"

"See what I mean by disgruntled?" said the Lord to Ageyutsa.

"Charlie, if you appear here, I can prove to you that this Archangel is special. She is one-of-a-kind!"

"You just say She? You just got to be pulling my leg. There ain't no such thing as a She Archangel."

"Then, call me a liar. Prove me wrong. Here's your chance!"

"You, lie? Well, that would be a first! Always telling the truth — the absolute truth, and nothing but the truth.

"Always pushing us cherubs around. I'll finish up in here. I'll even wash my hands. Lord, if you were going to reduce my powers like you did, the least you could have done was created toilet paper for us cherubs.

"Created the whole of all that is, but forgets to invent toilet paper.

"The little details count, Lord.

"It's the little details, like toilet paper, what makes life tolerable!"

There was a watery flushing sound from above and the sound of running tap water.

Then, in the middle of the room, as if a gateway had opened up, a low light to gradually increase its intensity, orange in color, began to radiate from a singular point and it began to grow larger in front of the Lord and Ageyutsa.

Ageyutsa began to shield her eyes, but the Lord gently pushed her hand down. Charlie always liked to make a grand entrance. She had nothing to fear.

Charlie stepped through the gateway from his 11 dimension realm into the four dimensions of the reality where the earth exists.

Charlie was very diminutive in his size, but he was larger than most cherubs, possessing dark, curly hair and a fat little tummy, much like a newborn baby, but he was extremely powerful, even though the Lord had limited his powers, due to their disagreements, which were many.

But, the Lord appreciated Charlie. He kept him in check. Charlie had a kind heart, underneath all the sarcasm.

The Lord had decided that since he would be too busy preparing to find Mordock, the sorcerer, that it would be Charlie who would train Ageyutsa in using her new powers and abilities as an Archangel.

Charlie was immediately met in the air by Hootie the owl.

There was an immediate confrontation beak to nose, but then Charlie realized that Hootie couldn't possibly be the Archangel. He then glanced to his right and there she stood, Ageyutsa, the female Archangel. She immediately caught his attention!?

"My Lord! What have you done?!? Your Father made Woman out of Man's rib and now you better him by making an Archangel out of a woman?"

Charlie began looking her over, from her feet all the way to the top of her head and he noticed her un-illuminated Halo.

"Your Halo ain't turned on. Don't tell me you're one of those women who —"

"Charlie, you behave with your language and manner. Her heart is still human. You are in the presence of a human woman — still. She is not a fully complete Archangel.

"Her heart was the only thing I couldn't change, or refused to, because of her free will as a human being. I had to respect that. It is my Father's unwritten law."

Charlie began looking her over in more detail, from head to foot, as he lit a cigar, much to the Lord's disapproval, but approximately 100 years ago, Charlie had met this fellow named Samuel Langhorne Clemens, better known as Mark Twain, they took a trip to Cuba in spirit form at Clemens' insistence, and after a few well rolled Havana's, Charlie had formed a habit.

"Lord, you may have made your first mistake, fashioning her from a woman. They are extremely emotional, argumentative, always crying and carrying on, over the littlest things."

The Lord smirked in his response, "Charlie, she hasn't said a blasted word to you. Not one blasted word, using your own language. You haven't given her a chance to say anything.

"It's all been about you. The way I look at it, you're the one who's been argumentative and carrying on over the littlest things. I think the two of you will be a perfect match for each other. You will complement each other well.

"Who knows — you might even learn something from her!

"I doubt she could possibly learn anything from a disgruntled cherub like you.

"I made her mostly for your benefit, not hers. Just who will be the student and you will be the teacher? We shall soon see.

"Now, if you don't mind — and even if you do mind — I need to change my appearance.

"I want to make myself presentable and I haven't been on earth in almost 2000 years. Perhaps if I removed the beard? That could confuse Mordock — hiding in plain sight like that. I need to disguise myself. Yes, that should be the answer.

"I need to disguise myself. So if you will excuse me, I shall take my leave of you both.

"Ageyutsa, thank you for your patience. I leave you in Charlie is questionably good hands."

"Lord, are you insulting me?"

"Charlie, if I have to answer that question for you, it will mean the cherubs aren't as smart as I thought they were.

"Of course I insulted you. But I didn't insult all cherubs, just you! Do I make myself clear?"

"Hmmph!"

Leaving Ageyutsa and Charlie to become better acquainted, the Lord departed remarking, "Well, what do you know? That cherub is getting smarter after all."

"Let's get something straight, Ageyutsa, you ain't human anymore — you are a Archangel.

"That means you operate in all 11 dimension. Humans operate in 4 dimensions — height, depth, length and time — but you operate in all 11. God and the Lord Jesus Christ, they got all 12 cylinders firing. They operated 12 dimensions, so don't mess with them.

"But, you are powerful beyond your wildest imagination. As a matter of fact, imagination and faith have everything to do with whatever an Archangel can do. They operate in 11 dimensions.

That's why you're heavier than you were. You were a human-butterfly, then a human-owl, then a human-Eagle.

All of those forms operate in 5 dimensions, bet you didn't know that. But now you do!

"Now, you're an Archangel.

"That means you got very special powers. You don't have to obey the physical laws of the universe, as an Archangel, them physical laws, of which there are too many to count, have to obey you.

"As a matter of fact, you can move planets and even the stars, once you get good enough about using your powers.

"You are spirit. Spirit has no limitations as far as size goes.

"That means you can be as small or as large as you need to be, at any given time.

"Whatever the situation requires.

"You are a Archangel.

"That means you are above the Angels. They operate in 10 dimensions, but you, being an Archangel, can operate in all 11.

"All physical laws must obey you, you don't obey them. They answer to you.

"Like I said, the Father and his son Jesus, they can get all 12 cylinders firing. They operate in that one extra dimension that you don't.

"And you don't go there! Is that understood, Ageyutsa?

"There was one guy that tried by the name Lucifer. And, we all know what happened in the end to him. So, no one wants to see you end up like him. Understood?

"Know your limitations, girl, Ageyutsa, or whatever you want to call yourself."

CHAPTER 13
BASIC TRAINING

(For Female Archangels, as described and prescribed, by Charlie the Cherub)

Where does one train an Archangel? Not on the earth. Archangels are celestial beings. They need to branch out and visit other worlds. We do live in a solar *system*. There are other planets.

As far as planets go, Pluto was downgraded to a dwarf planet in the year 2006. It was too small to serve any useful purpose. It was no challenge at all.

That Left 8 Planets in Our Solar System — and Charlie chose this planet, Ageyutsa's training ground, well, very well.

He chose the planet Uranus. The planet Uranus is the seventh planet from the sun. It is the weirdo of the 8 known planets in our solar system because it is tilted over on its side at 97 degrees to the horizontal.

Supposedly, it was struck by another planet while in its formation many billions of years ago.

A single year around the sun for this planet is 84 of our own. Its North Pole usually directly faces the sun. Wind speeds typically reach nearly 700 miles per hour. It is four times the size of the earth, roughly, in volume. It is one of the gas giants. It smells like a huge fart!

It has 27 moons, 5 very large ones, and a very dark 3-ring system, much like Saturn. It has an average surface temperature of less than 355 degrees below zero.

Pressures in the lower atmosphere, consisting mostly of liquid methane, nitrogen and defused carbon dioxide gases, the gaseous mixtures are why it smells like a huge fart, and are 100 times as a great as those found at the bottom of the Pacific, heating its interior to over 4000 degrees and crushing the carbon in the atmosphere sufficiently to make it rain diamonds.

Earth is in the Goldilocks Zone, where life flourishes.

Welcome to a real Hell, except we are no longer on Earth, we are on Uranus over 1.6 billion miles away from the earth.

It is also excellent training ground for new archangels, be they male or female, or neither, in order to hone their skills and abilities which can control weather systems and all of the elements, especially with the elements and weather systems that are so wild and so non-earth-like.

That distance made it safe enough, Charlie hoped, for Ageyutsa to learn about her new powers and abilities as an Archangel.

As both Ageyutsa and Charlie descended through the upper atmosphere of Uranus, Ageyutsa became frightened beyond all measure. But, her fear began to slowly subside when she soon realized that she wasn't feeling the cold.

The diamonds in the atmosphere that were forming now that she was entering the interior of the planet, although the diamonds were projectiles traveling as fast as bullets, fascinated her and they were not harming her, they were passing through her, for an Arch-angel is spirit and she was unharmed.

She was spirit. She was no longer human. All Charlie had to do was convince her that it was so.

"Ageyutsa, stop being so afraid. Stop thinking like a human. You're not human anymore, you are a Archangel.

"Remember what I told you. You control all physical laws of the universe, they obey you. You don't obey them. The physical laws of the universe obey you. You are a Archangel! Start acting like one. Girl, you just don't realize how powerful you really are.

"When you were part human and part eagle, you operated in 5 dimensions. You were a magical being. But archangels operate in 11 dimensions. You are far more than magical now. You are a Archangel.

"I saw you battle with Mordock when you were in your eagle form, but he cleaned your clock!

"Why? Because he is an Archangel, operating in 11 dimensions, and you could only operate in 5, 6 at best. But now you are his equal.

"Always remember this, Ageyutsa: you are an Archangel of life. Whereas, Mordock is an Archangel of death. Life is always stronger than death. The Lord made that so when he died on the cross and proved it, and he also made you!

"You are more powerful, in your present form, as a female Archangel, than Mordock or even his father Lucifer!

"A female always represents life. You as a female Archangel must represent life.

"Mordock and his father Lucifer — they are archangels of death. But you are an Archangel of life. And life is always stronger than death.

"I brought you to this planet to test your abilities to their fullest. To test your faith in the Lord and his father, God.

"Your strength lies in your faith both in yourself and in the Almighty from where you draw your power.

"Always remember that, Ageyutsa. Always remember that — above all else. Your greatest strength always comes through God! Not yourself, but through God and the Lord Jesus Christ his Son.

"The Lord has given you an opportunity to show your appreciation for his gift to you. The Lord has limitless power, but it is only through its proper usage that you truly glorify him.

"Now, as the very first female Archangel of the Lord, exert your control over this planet. You can move planets. You can move even the stars. As an Archangel, God will grant you that much power.

"This planet is over on its side at 97 degrees to the horizontal. Tilt it back up to 23.5 degrees to the horizontal to match Earth. Right the planet!

"Alter it seasons, calm these winds, change the atmosphere.

"Make oceans of freshwater. Make land and move it up through the waters to form continents.

"This planet is cold. Warm it! Change the atmosphere to produce a greenhouse effect to warm it. Make this planet a paradise.

"Since this planet has no core, make one! Build your own core and move it. Turn this planet the right way up. Start acting like an Archangel. Stop thinking like a scared, weak human being.

"You are far more than human now — you are a moving spirit, move upon this planet as a spirit.

"You are an Archangel. You control the elements, they do not control you! You are the boss. You are in charge. Act it!

"And, if God does not respond to your prayer, it's because he wants to see what you're capable of doing on your own.

"He gave you all that you need. He has given you the power, Archangel, now build this world.

"Reshape it into a paradise. The laws of the universe are waiting for your commands. The Lord God will not wait forever.

"What he's asking you to do is simple — for an Archangel.

"He built the planets and the moons and the stars and this whole universe from nothing in the Beginning. From nothing!

"You got it easy! He's given you a planet — this planet — rebuild it, reshape it, reform it! Make it your own paradise! Bring life to it! Any form of life you wish. It's up to you and God is waiting to see what you do. Don't disappoint Him."

CHAPTER 14

AGEYUTSA'S NEW WORLD

There is a misconception about God. God is not always serious. God does have a sense a humor. Putting Charlie in charge of Ageyutsa, God was very pleased and he smiled.

In fact, he downright laughed out loud and the heavens nearly shook from his pleasure that he took from watching these two misfits.

Ageyutsa had no idea of what she was doing and Charlie was downright militant it is approach, almost like a sergeant major, yelling and screaming and shouting at the top of his lungs over those 300 mile an hour winds on the planet Uranus. But, Ageyutsa was learning.

The first thing Charlie had to do was to adjust Ageyutsa's Halo. This was like a radio antenna, directly connecting her to God. Charlie couldn't get the frequency quite right. He tried low power. That didn't quite work. Then he moved it up to medium power. The Halo began to glow.

Ageyutsa could feel God's sheer, absolute joy and his creative power flowing through her was like tickling her. The more juice Charlie allowed to flow through the antenna, through the Halo, the more Ageyutsa laughed in response.

Charlie was in back of Ageyutsa, making the final, minor adjustments. It was like adjusting an antenna in many ways –

Charlie got a bit of a shock from the power flowing through the Halo. He almost cursed several times directly above himself, not that it made a difference, talking to God, from below, to the side or up above, for God was everywhere and God was seeing everything.

He was impressed by Charlie. Charlie was controlling his temper for the first time in nearly a century.

God understood now in bringing these two together had been a very good thing to do. They complemented each other, even though their personalities were like fire and ice. Charlie was definitely on fire — literally! His robe had been caught aflame from the energy God was transmitting down from heaven. God did it as a bit of a joke, just to get a jolt into Charlie, and he certainly had succeeded in doing that.

The first thing Ageyutsa did as an Archangel was to form a core to the planet Uranus. The planet was technically a gas giant, meaning it had no solid core.

She began grabbing diamonds out of the air, diamonds that were forming like droplets. Ageyutsa always appreciated shiny things like diamonds. She took out the diamonds from the surrounding 300 mile an hour winds as if picking blueberries from a bush.

It was in this next phase where she learned of her great strength. Diamond is the hardest known substance in the universe.

Yet, it was like putty in her hands and she molded the diamonds together under great heat and great pressure being exerted through her hands. She worked rapidly, collecting the diamonds and merging them into the central core she was developing. The diamond core was as large as the Empire State building and rapidly growing from its early beginnings.

Finally, when the diamond core was several miles thick, Ageyutsa stopped adding to the core. The job was complete. She passed her hand completely around and she flew around the diamond core.

This next phase locked the diamond core into the very physics of the planet. Now, if the core moved, so did the planet in its entirety and she righted the planet, pulling it up from its 97 degrees horizontal tilt until the planet was almost vertical. She did not warn Charlie of this maneuver and Charlie plunged into the 4000 degrees just below them both, slightly singeing his rear end upon contact.

God must've been heard laughing out loud throughout the heavens as he watched Charlie's contortions.

God muttered under his breath, "Serves him right."

And he literally roared once more, giving Ageyutsa even more power and energy to deal with through her Halo.

That Halo was shining as bright as a miniature nova during a star's formation. It would've been visible from Earth had the astronomers had had their telescopes pointed in the planet's direction.

Uranus already had a bluish-green color to it, but the Green was slowly dissipating and so were the winds.

With her arms spread wide in a cross position, Ageyutsa was literally pushing the winds back and calming them. No longer was there 300 mile an hour hurricanes, but calm, warming breezes being generated from the planet's core of 4000 degrees.

Ageyutsa was literally producing an internal heat source for the planet to warm itself. It would be like a Franklin stove heating a room.

The icy temperatures of nearly 355 degrees below zero were rapidly climbing. It was now above the zero mark.

Uranus was becoming Earth-like and it shone like a blue jewel, a planet transitioning into a habitable paradise.

God raised an eyebrow in approval and he was impressed. It reminded him of when he created the earth so many millennia ago.

This little Archangel, Ageyutsa, she was doing all that was right in his eyes — even though Charlie was violently protesting, telling her to slow down, to make things easier!

"Who do you think you are? You think you're God? Slow down, Ageyutsa.

"God took six days to create a world — hell, you're doing it all in one! Let me look at what you're doing. Yeah. Yeah. You got it right. Downright pleasant. Get rid and that damned hard core! Put some grass on it!"

"Charlie!" God said, "watch that language!"

"Lord, she's moving too fast. She has no idea what she's doin'."

"It's looking good to me, Charlie. She has my approval."

"Well, she ain't got mine! Why don't you come down here?"

"What, and break up a perfectly good fight that you two have going? I haven't seen this much fun in a million years!"

"Lord, I can't even light my cigar! Ain't got time to smoke it. That little Archangel down here, first it's one thing, then it's another.

"Brought up a kind of new, fresh kind of seawater — full of minerals that ain't found on earth, gives it a sparkling glow like I've never seen — as a matter-of-fact it was an entire ocean as big as the Atlantic on Earth — from the core of the planet!

"Then, she turns around and transforms all that methane in the atmosphere into H2O.

"Completely transformed the color of the planet, without my having to tell her how to do it.

"She just does it without askin'.

"I can't keep up! She's younger than I am!"

"Ah-ah, Charlie, young minds, fresh ideas! I kind of like it," replied the Almighty.

"Can you just imagine the new life that will take place in that new ocean, Charlie?"

"Holy —! Don't give her any other, new ideas, Lord. That crazy Archangel. She's crazy, you know!"

"I say she's doing just fine. You live with it, Charlie. You can live with it.

"Let's turn her up another notch, shall we? Ageyutsa, we're going to shift you into the Most High gear. Let's see what you can really do!"

CHAPTER 15

REPORT CARD

With Uranus now a tropical paradise, it was Charlie who told her to cease her Archangel efforts on transforming the planet.

He had to fill out a report and pass it directly to God for his approval.

"Let's see... Overall average temperature the planet — now a pleasant 72 degrees. Hmmm... Rather pleasant — pass!

"Magnetic field now fully locked on both poles — successful. Pass!

"Central heating now in place using planet's core. Very much needed now that we are situated 1.7 million miles from the sun. Fully in place, 98 % efficient and operational. Good.

"Specific gravity of the planet still at 89 % of Earth's gravity. Excellent. Planet tilt moved from 97 degrees to 23.5 degrees. Good. Seasons now in effect.

"Planet core now a fully established and stabilized. Good.

"Planet no longer smells like a huge fart in space! Excellent.

"Moons. Let's see...1,2,3,4... Carry the 1... Wait a minute! I only count 22 moons. There were 27 of them! Where did the five large ones go? I don't see them anywhere! Wait a minute!

"Ageyutsa, just what in the hell is that electrified sac behind you?!? I never told you to — you stole them! I don't believe you! Once a thief, always a thief!

"You actually think you could get away with stealing five moons from a planet without my noticing?"

"But these five biggest ones are the prettiest. And, Earth could use five more moons. I mean, they would be so pretty in the sky. Earth only has one. It needs more! Please allow me to bring these five big ones back — for souvenirs — from my big trip to the Uranus!"

"Ageyutsa, I don't believe you! You are a Archangel and yet you don't understand the basic physics and Celestial mechanics and purpose of moons?

"Can you just imagine the chaos of adding five more moons to the one that's already there for the earth? The tides on the earth would be absolutely humongous!

"All the fishes and birds would be goin' crazy, not to mention the daytimes and nighttimes. It would disturb every rhythm on the face of the planet.

"People wouldn't even know when to sleep. First it would be night-time, then daytime, then night-time again.

"Oh, you are definitely a woman! Always picking out the big, glittering ones — the biggest ones at that!"

"Charlie, I just wanted to —!"

"Oh, for all that's holy! Here come the damned tears! Waterworks from an Archangel! Female Archangel! Absolutely no doubt about it now! Shut them tears off — and put those moons back! This instant!

"And re-stabilize the planet once you do.

"I'm not going to show you a second time because I know you know how to do it. Put 'em back!

"You put those moons back exactly the way you found them — and I do mean EXACTLY!

"It's a darn good thing we didn't bring those five moons with us all the way to the earth!

"Probably would've destabilized the entire planet! Archangels! They have absolutely no concept — of how this blasted universe works, they just do, without even thinking about what they are doin'.

"Just for that — I'm taking five marks off! You ain't perfect! I just knew it was too good to be true!

"You're a thief underneath it all. Always were, always will be! Human heart! It's that human heart beatin' in your chest.

"You're still part human! I got me a part human, part Archangel thief!"

"A thief for a Archangel!!! A Archangel with the human heart! A human heart that still likes to steal! If it glitters, she's gonna take it!"

CHAPTER 16

ARMAGEDDON – EARTH

Planet Earth — condition: World War III — Armageddon!

In Charlie's and Ageyutsa's absence, Captain Archibald Crane had upgraded the *HMS Venture* to 21st century standards, equipping the ship for battle with nuclear warheads. All aircraft carriers, battleships, land tanks, all submarines with nuclear capability and conventional weaponry was brought into service. They were battling a fallen archangel by the name of Mordock, Enchantra and other fallen Angels, impish elves.

All had been released from the very center of the earth after Mordock had grown to a size even greater than the planet Earth itself.

He stood there, menacingly hovering above the Earth, his sword withdrawn and having pierced through both poles of the planet, he had impaled it from the very North to the South, all the way through.

Normally, Earth is a paradise, in the garden spot of the solar system, with very mild winds by comparison to the other planets, orbiting about its single star in the "Goldilocks Zone" where life normally flourishes and thrives.

The planet Earth's rotation had been halted. The earth stood in space deadly still. The earth normally turns at over 1000 miles per hour, as it has a circumference of over 25,000 miles in circumference and a full rotation of the globe amounts to 24 hours.

Halt the rotation of any planet, and any atmosphere, the very winds of the planet, remain in motion at those former rotational speeds.

The earth was experiencing hurricanes of over 1000 miles per hour over the entire globe.

The United States of America and, indeed, all of North America was no longer recognizable. A larger landmass, larger than the surface area of the entire country had been thrust up through the earth's mantle. It was the land of Eden, which had been hidden by God, many millennia earlier, before the Great Flood of Noah.

We live on a water world. Over 72 percent of the earth's surface is liquid. Antarctica and the northern regions of the

Arctic are solid masses of ice, but such ice will drift when the entire rotation of the world has stopped and this is precisely what was happening.

The Lord Jesus Christ was in combat with Mordock, himself growing to a size equal to his archangel rival. They were struggling in physical combat above the world.

It was the site of horror beyond anything either Charlie or Ageyutsa had ever witnessed in their lifetimes or beyond them. Ageyutsa, from space, cast a quick glance down to the surface of the planet in search of Hootie. With the sharpening eyes of an eagle, she scanned the surface of the world, of the land that was once her country, the United States of America — which now had a massive, super volcano thrust up through it's very center as a consequence of the rising of Eden beneath it.

Ageyutsa was heard to whisper under her breath, "Oh my God! No! Hootie! Charlie, stay here to help the Lord. I must return to the earth — now! Hootie is — I can't say it!"

Shrinking to the size of a normal woman, although still retaining archangel wings, Ageyutsa returned to the earth to find the lifeless body of Hootie.

She was met by Captain Archibald Crane, whose ship had been scuttled on the rising ocean waters on a new shoreline that had formed when the earth had stopped rotating. The good Captain explained to Ageyutsa that Hootie had been struck by lightning, a black lightning and had been struck down by Mordock. The body of the huge owl remained lifeless on the ground before her. There was no breath. There was no sign of life. Hootie had been killed in a cataclysmic battle with the archangel Mordock.

"His last words to me, ma'am, was that he wanted to defend your honor and Eden's in your absence.

"It was his duty and his honor to serve with you over these last few months as you patrolled Eden together."

Ageyutsa glared skyward at the massive shadows of the Lord and Mordock.

Her eyes were turning fiery red with rage, the rage of an archangel being brought to the surface and she felt the almost limitless power of God-like energy flow through her veins for the very first time.

"Lord, how can you permit this — this needless death? Whether it is your will, or even if it isn't, the monster Mordock must be destroyed. I am not killing a man, I am destroying the monster!

"He is not human, nor am I any longer! Thou Shalt Not Kill? That applies to only humans — and I am no longer human.

"Fellow archangel, prepare to meet thy doom!"

She launched herself from the planet Earth, growing to the size of a mountain and then much greater, much, much greater.

Mordock had his back to the earth and to what was coming up from its surface. He did not see Ageyutsa, as she approached him from his blindside with his back to her.

She withdrew her sword. The very first time she had ever used it since becoming an archangel.

She used her butterfly capabilities to telepathically communicate with both the Lord and Mordock in outer space as she left the atmosphere of the planet behind her.

She thrust her sword through the back of Mordock from behind him.

She exclaimed, "If the Lord will not kill you, and prefers just toying with you here in space, Mordock, then try my blade!

"You will not receive such mercies from me, you bastard from hell!"

CHAPTER 17

ARMAGEDDON – URANUS

Mordock and Ageyutsa were both archangels. Both were of roughly equal strength and their powers and abilities were the same. One Archangel, Mordock, drew his strength from his father, Satan. The other Archangel, Ageyutsa, drew her strength from God.

It was the ultimate and final clash between Evil and Good, with all of humanity's and Earth's existence hanging in the balance on the outcome.

Just how would an Archangel kill another Archangel? It would be a battle to the death of one.

The battle for Earth would not be fought on the earth, but on the planet Uranus, the planet which Ageyutsa had transformed into a jewel-like paradise, the insurance policy that was put in place by God by allowing Ageyutsa to learn of her strengths and weaknesses as the first female Archangel.

By the cherub Charlie's choosing, this had been the training ground for Ageyutsa to begin honing her skills, learning of her abilities, learning of the power of faith in God and the creativity gifted to her by God that had channeled through her as she had made Uranus earth-like.

She rapidly descended from the planet's orbit, still clutching, tightly clutching her struggling foe, Mordock, whose lungs now filled with air and could now be heard screaming as they descended through the atmospheric layers of this alien world.

They both crashed heavily into the surface of the world, much like a huge meteor, they had left a massive crater on the surface of the planet.

Ageyutsa was the first to get to her feet and while Mordock did make a lunge at her on the ground, she was already airborne and rapidly ascending above him.

Her eyes glowed red out of sheer revenge and she circled overhead from high above.

"You were about to strike the Lord, with your big weapon, your mighty sword, and kill him once more on the earth.

"You murdered Hootie, you stopped the rotation of the earth, leaving nearly 8,000,000,000 to die, and you don't care! All you bring about is death! Death and control!

"You are just like your father. It was all about power and control for him. It's all about power and control for you.

"I will show you what real power is! I will show you what real control is — welcome to my world.

"Here, I am God! This is my world! And I judge you! He was a simple, magical owl named Hootie. He was no match for you. You are nothing but a huge bully!

"Try me! Try me on my world, Mordock! I am not a defensive foul on the earth. I am an Archangel of the universe, and of God.

"Feel my wrath, fellow Archangel! All that you see before you was once the planet Uranus. Now, this is my world. I created all of this, all that you see before you, and beyond your sight.

"Here, I am God!

"Here, I judge you — for who and what you really are — an evil and wicked sorcerer, nothing but a bully, and I find you guilty!

"I banished you to this world — forever — for all of eternity! If you can even survive its true nature!

"What you see before you is all an illusion. It's not real. And the illusion ends now!

"Feel this planet for what it truly is — an off-centered, twisted, demented, warped bully, just as twisted and perverted as you!

"As its creator, as God here on this world, I say, let this planet serve a useful purpose — let it be your tomb! The illusion ends now! Feel my wrath! Welcome to *my* Hell! Welcome to *my* own lake of fire, Archangel!

Mordock growled in defiance at her, righted himself on the planet's surface and began to take flight, but he was hit by 50,000 miles of 300 mile an hour winds. The blue sky which it lit the entire planet rapidly darkened, the sun was nothing more than a distant, ever-dimming light in the sky. The pleasant temperatures on the surface began to rapidly drop.

It was like being trapped at the bottom of the Pacific Ocean, only 100 times worse, for such were the pressures on this much larger planet Uranus.

It hit him like a wall. Just like running into a wall, a brick wall, impenetrable and ever pressing downward, the absolute, sheer weight of the atmosphere drove him into the very core of the planet, a diamond core that was rapidly disintegrating from the enormous pressures from all around.

There was no longer any solid core. The planet was once again turning into a gaseous giant. Lightning storms began to form all throughout the ever thickening atmosphere, each more 500 times more intense than any that ever to exist on earth. He began to sink into it. There was no longer anything solid to latch onto or stand upon. He was in a massive see 50,000 miles thick of nothing but poisonous gas.

He was in the very center of his all too-rapidly transforming planet and its core began to heat up once more to over 4000 degrees centigrade, as the last of the diamond core, once placed there and hand built by Ageyutsa, began its final phase of disintegration as it dissipated.

The last of Ageyutsa's illusion was no more.

Mordock felt the ever-growing pressures on and throughout his entire body building. Mere instances in time felt like centuries under the enormous weight in pressures of the Uranus unrelenting atmosphere.

He smelled sulfur. He smelled the suffocating hydrocarbons. There was very little oxygen. He smelled magnesium.

And all he could see above, below and to all sides was black — ever darkening black — above and all around. He felt the enormous heat and he could hear her words echoing from high above.

He could see her red eyes, glowing above the thunder and lightning flashes, much like a growing fire, a growing fire that was now beneath him as the last of the grass and green lushness that once encircled the globe was left adrift and being turned into flame.

He heard her last words, as he was crushed out of existence, imploding, "Welcome to your last home, in *my* Hell — Burn, Archangel, burn!!!

"The illusion that once was is no more. Welcome to *my* world, Mordock, the murderer! BUUUURRRRNNN!!!"

The planet Uranus began to keel over into its original configuration on its side, its North Pole once again facing the sun.

CHAPTER 18

MIRACLES

From orbit around the planet, Ageyutsa visualized the entire planet between her hands and with a last rotating motion and movement of her hands through the void of space, the planet move back to, settled and locked into its original 97 degree position.

Uranus was now fully restored to its original orientation in space and the sorcerer, the son of Satan, Mordock, remains trapped at the very center of the planet, crushed into nonexistence by the sheer weight in pressures of the thousands upon thousands of miles of poisonous atmosphere.

Ageyutsa, seeing all that was done was finished in good, flew off in the direction of the planet Earth. The rotation of that planet had been halted by Mordock's impaling the earth.

The Lord would need her help. The Lord would handle the bigger picture, by healing the Earth. Of this, Ageyutsa was quite certain. Where she had faith in the Lord. But even the Lord, cannot do everything alone. She would have to take care of the details.

Upon her return at the majestic magical Archangel as large as a mountain, the Lord instructed her and charged her with restoring the globe.

When the planet was originally created, it was done in six days. They did not have six days. The earth's rotation had stopped. They had mere hours to restore it to normal.

With her halo now fully charged by the Lord, he communicated telepathically with her, instructing her on what to do. She grew even larger and she flew faster, while thrusting each of her arms through the deep oceans of the planet. Here, she telepathically communicated, using her retain butterfly capabilities, with all the fishes of the sea, with all the whales and everything that swam in the waters.

She reassured them and pushed back the great tidal waters of each of the great oceans, calming them, restoring tranquility to three quarters of the globe through this action.

She pushed the California coastline back into its place. California was no longer an island, but once again restored to the mainland of the United States.

She flew at hypersonic speed, faster and faster, approaching the speed of light and she circled the globe at a rate of 25 times per second, calming the shorelines by the sonic booms that were being created all over the world by her rapid accelerations.

She met the Lord in geosynchronous orbit around the world. Here, he instructed her, as he did.

Each blew light, warm breaths as mighty giants of the heavens. Each so large, that they both held the entire world together as if it was no more than a large, blue marble in their hands.

Rotation of the earth once again was restored, and set back in its orbit, ever so gradually, and ever so gently by the Lord and Ageyutsa. The high winds once again ceased and were calmed as both the Lord and Ageyutsa spread their arms over the lands and the waters that was the planet Earth.

Ageyutsa, as an Archangel of life, placed her hand over the wound inflicted by the sword of Mordock and the wound was instantly healed.

The passageway to the surface world had been sealed, trapping the fallen Angels, the gnomes and the elves deep within the planet.

Both the Lord and Ageyutsa gently floated back down to the earth and set foot upon solid ground once more.

Ageyutsa approached the lifeless body of Hootie. She gently lifted him from the ground and cuddled him. The owl remained lifeless. Tears began to flow from Ageyutsa.

"Please, dear Lord, please restore his life. Make them as he once was."

"I will not do that, Ageyutsa — you will!"

"No, I cannot do that. Only you can restore life. Only you have beaten death. Conquer death one last time for this darling owl, my dearest friend and companion. Now I know my heart is still human, because it is breaking."

"It is so written that I shall dry all the tears of the world. Watch and learn, Ageyutsa, of your true power is a female Archangel of life, not of death. All I need from you, Ageyutsa, if you will allow me, please let me wipe away your tears and your sadness — and watch and learn of your greatest gift from my Father!

"You are an Archangel of life. These tears I wipe away from you are the tears of an Archangel. They have very special, life-giving properties, then only you possess. Watch. If I place my wetted hand near your loving companion Hootie's beak."

Hootie's eyes began to flutter. His chest began to rise and descend as the special and unique chemicals of an Archangel's tears, the very first female Archangel's tears, were drunken in by her feathered companion.

He yawned as if awakening from a silent sleep. He smiled.

"Ageyutsa! Ageyutsa, are you alright? Ageyutsa — safe from that most wicked Mordock?"

"Hootie! Oh my God! Hootie, you're alive! Just look at you. There's not a mark on you!

"Oh, Hootie, I love you so much! So very much! Never, ever try to defend me again! I can't risk ever losing you again, you lovely, adorable creature!"

"I love you, Ageyutsa!"

Almost the end, but not quite. You see, there was one unmentioned side benefit to being an Archangel, an Archangel of life, in the presence of the Lord —Ageyutsa, who had forgotten her name early on in this story, was restored her full memory. Ageyutsa was not truly just Ageyutsa, for the Lord knew her name all along and restored her name onto her through His blessing. Ageyutsa's real, human name was actually ________.

You, the reader, need to take a moment and decide Ageyutsa's human name of the earth.

The End

Printed in the United States
By Bookmasters